HAPPY BIRTHDAY
MARIA
WITH LOVE
FROM
ENRICO & ALINE

First published in Great
Britain in 2000 by
PAVILION BOOKS LIMITED
London House,
Great Eastern Wharf
Parkgate Road, London
SW11 4NQ
www.pavilionbooks.co.uk

Designed by
Stafford Cliff

Production Artwork by
Matt Sarraf

Andrew Martin photography
by Dominic Blackmore

Picture research by
Jess Walton

A CIP catalogue record for
this book is available
from the British Library.

ISBN 1 86205 3820

Printed and bound in Italy
by de Agostini
Originated by Alliance
Graphics, Bedford and
Singapore

10 9 8 7 6 5 4 3 2 1

This book can be ordered
direct from the publisher.
Please contact
the Marketing Department.
But try your bookshop first.

ANDREW MARTIN

Fusion
Interiors

Martin Waller &
Dominic Bradbury

PAVILION

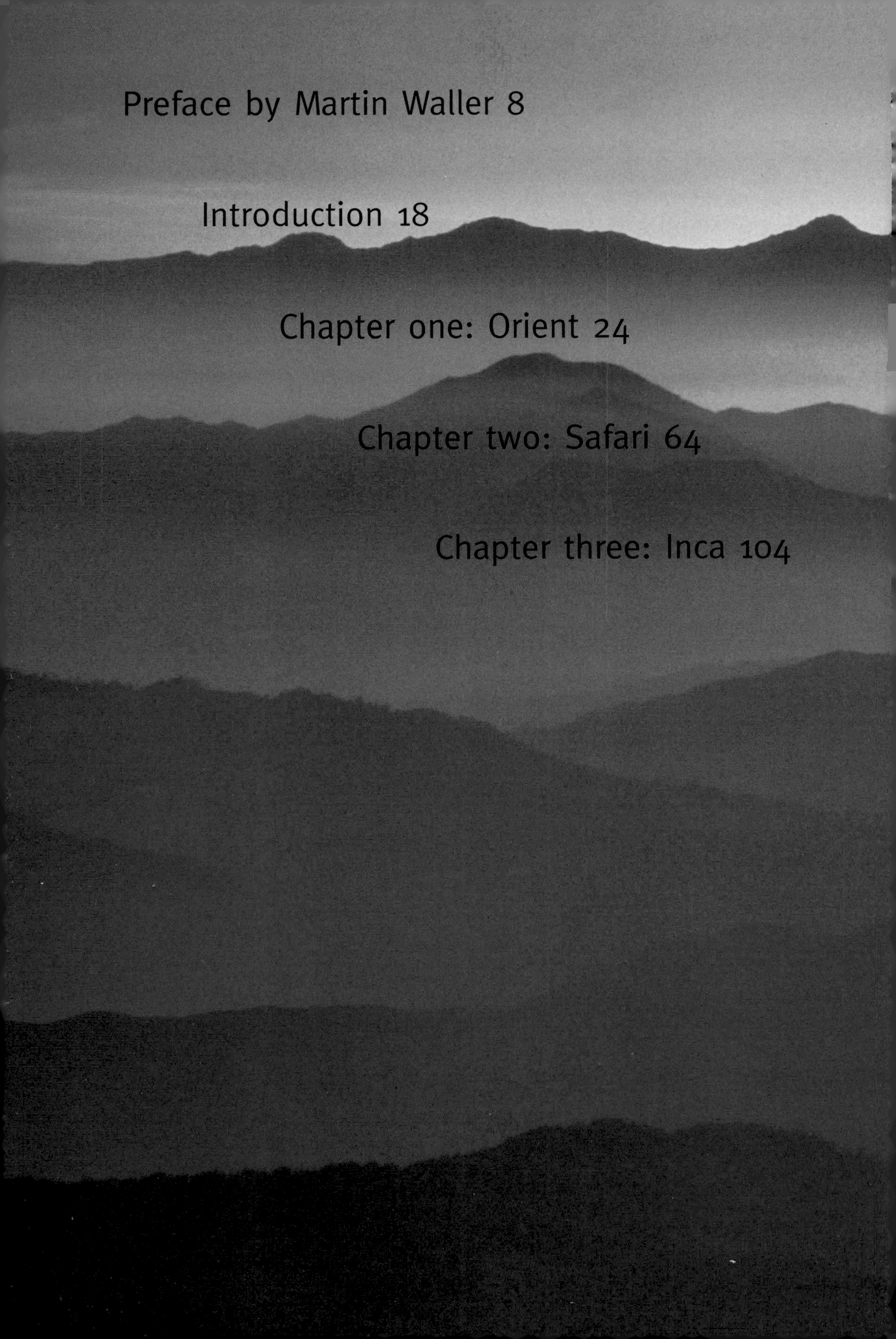

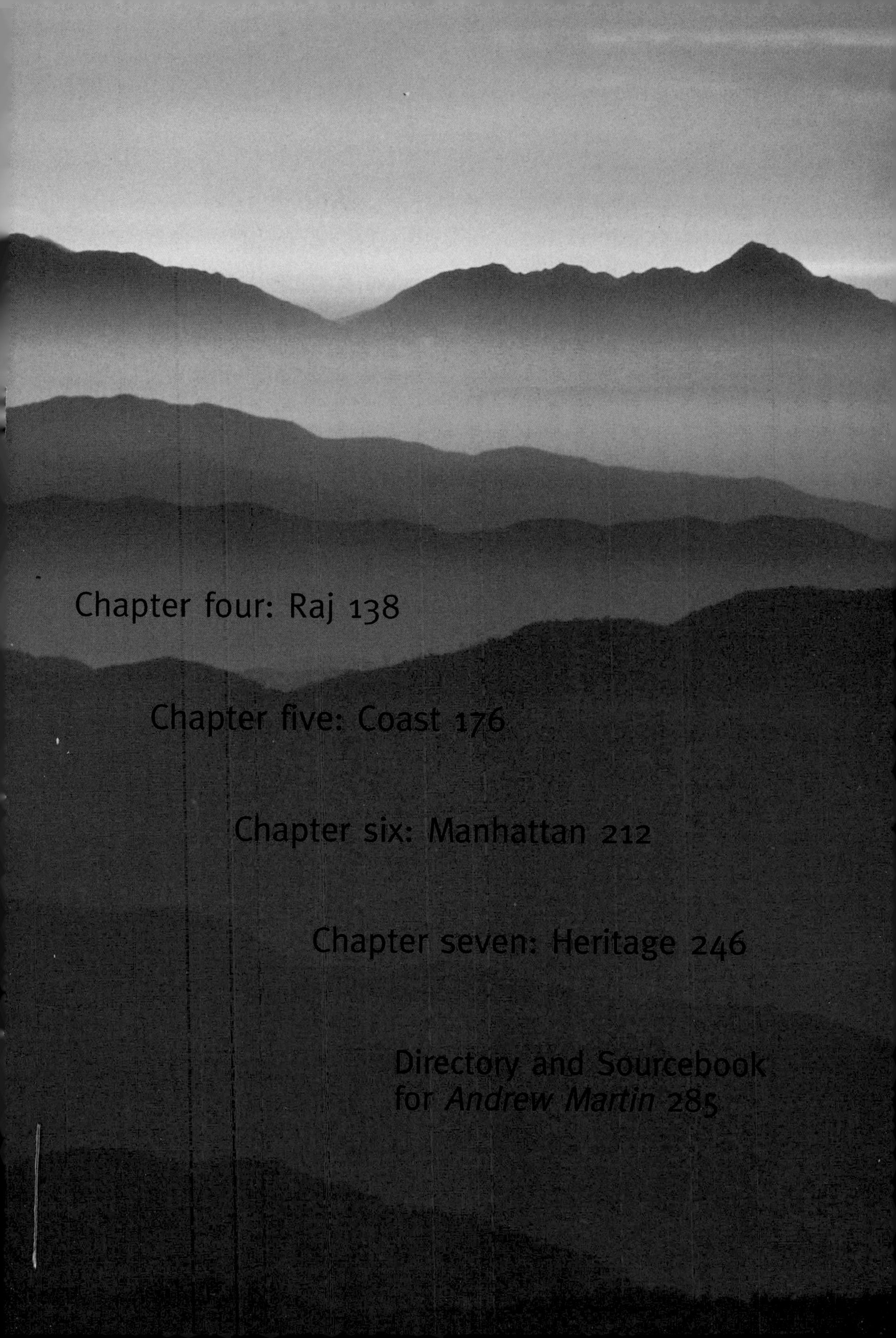

Martin Waller
Preface

Travel is the great luxury of our generation. We take for granted trips to far-flung places that our forefathers would have thought extraordinary. It took Marco Polo 17 years to make his famous trip to China. You could have breakfast in Beijing tomorrow.

This gift of travel has given us the opportunity to see and absorb cultures so different from our own. We can see for ourselves wonders that were previously just thought to be travellers' tall tales.

The reverse side is that the world's differences are blurring. Whole cultures, and even peoples, are disappearing. In the final decades of the nineteenth century the lifestyle of the native American was almost wiped out. At the start of the twentieth century aborigines and pygmies were still being hunted. Even today, the Amazonian Indian is under extreme threat. It is ironic that just at the point when these cultures are staring at oblivion, people are realizing their value. A common culture underpinned by international media and worldwide brands may or may not create the beneficial effect of bringing harmony and common understanding, but it certainly will make the world far less interesting.

I don't doubt that the world will continue to shrink. We can see it close to home as crofters in Scotland, tin miners in Cornwall, and family farmers in rural America see their age-old ways of life disappearing. Perhaps we are at a junction where, although travel has become straightforward, mass communication has not yet destroyed the whole point of travel.

Design has always been about more than just attractive patterns. It is about reflecting a personal view on a subject. For me this has often been about describing my love of various places and peoples. It was in Thailand that I first saw the miracle of silk yarn production and the laborious work of ikat weaving, which can take a day to produce a single metre. But it was more than just the end product that captivated me; it was the serene patience of the weavers, the skill of the dyers and the ancient tradition of the technique. This was what set me on the road to developing our various fabric designs for Andrew Martin.

With a fickle heart I have fallen in love with many products in this way: pottery in China, rattan in the Philippines, wood-carvings in India, rugs in Tibet. I cannot resist the product on account of the culture that has created it. And it's not just true in exotic places. The United States, which I have always enjoyed, is also a constant source of inspiration, ranging from the sophistication of New York to the more wholesome look of the 1950s.

My designs for Andrew Martin are infused with this attitude. I think it's common for designers in any field to want to communicate something. For the Bauhaus it was about a new attitude towards form and function. Often a political viewpoint has been an influence, and religion even more so. And love has always been a powerful motivator with much influence.

For me design has been about reflecting different cultures and communicating a passion for the peoples that made them. While many designers want to say something new, I want to say something old – to capture a flavour of an antique land and somehow bottle it. It's a homage to the many generations from different lands who have bequeathed a legacy of design.

Introduction

There's a rich vein of talk in the world of

interior design about style, elegance, even comfort. But a fourth prime principle has to be escapism and the value of escapism is always underplayed. It is, however, one of the most important aspects of home living: when we walk through the front door we want to forget about the endless routines of everyday life and all of the pressures and frustrations which they bring. We want to escape, and to escape with style, elegance, and in comfort.

Escapism lies at the heart of *Fusion Interiors*, which brings together eclectic influences from around the world into a cohesive and natural look. Just as we leave our worries about everyday concerns behind us when we travel – drinking in strange new cities and landscapes, colours and crafts, people and provinces – so we want to find a similar sense of escape in the haven of the home. We can do this through the value of association, whether it be with rich colours that remind us of a particular place, translucent ceramics, a richly woven fabric, a vibrant tribal pattern or something as simple as a texture like that of raffia, silk or lacquer sheen. So many choices in the design of the home offer opportunities to escape by association, to create some connection with another culture, another time and place.

The growth of international travel has completely altered the way we look at the world. The freedom to travel and increasing accessibility to its many pleasures have opened up endless possibilities for discovery and adventure that would have been impossible for the silent majority a few generations ago.

We can step onto a plane and within hours be walking the crowded souks of Marrakesh, staring in wonder at the Terracotta Army of the Emperor Qin in Xian, China, or wandering among the ruins of great Mayan temples on the Yucatán Peninsula.

This freedom to travel is something many of us now take for granted, but the mental snapshots we bring back from every journey often have a profound influence. The cool simplicity of white clapboard houses on the shores of the island of Nantucket, crisp in the sunshine. The sight of a small boy on the back of a buffalo splashing through a lush green paddy field, glimpsed from a train as it carries you through the heart of Thailand. Or the monumental grey stone head of a broken statue, ancient and worn, covered in emerald creepers and stumbled upon among the ruins of an Orissa temple.

These are snapshots in time, images that take you back instantly to another part of the world, reviving a reassuring, intoxicating sense of discovery. And just as we bring back memories and photographs, so we also bring back influences and ideas, inspiration and excitement. Sometimes it might be a simple passion for a shade, tone or texture seen in the glaze of celadon ceramics from Thailand or the glaze of zelliges tiles, with their traditional Moroccan patterns, in a Maghreb hammam – the ornately tiled baths common to the region. It might be something greater and more physical: intensely coloured lacquerware trays or jewellery boxes from Japan; bold and bright Indonesian batiks, hand crafted and wrapped in rice paper; saris from a Jaipur market, smelling of cinnamon and dust. Treasures in themselves, rich in connections with a particular place and people. Elements of style and savoured tastes of another culture and another way of living.

Of course the whole idea of being shaped by the designs and crafts of other countries is nothing new. From the days of the early silk roads that wound from the Mediterranean through Persia and into China, there has been traffic from East to West and West to East. Myriad spice routes and camel trains traversed the Sahara or snaked across India's endless Thar Desert.

Since the sixteenth century, when regular trade links between Europe and the Orient were being established, there has been a fascination with the crafts and skills of far-off places. In Europe it was an interest not just in tea and spices but textiles, porcelain and lacquerware. By the seventeenth century the craftsmanship of Japanese and Chinese artisans was having a solid impact upon the homes of wealthy Europeans and chinoiserie, japanning (or lacquering) and fine silks were in fashion.

One only has to look at Brighton Pavilion in Sussex, England, to see the power of the Oriental influence upon the West by the early nineteenth century. Architect John Nash designed the Pavilion as a Moghul fantasy for his royal patron, the Prince Regent (later George IV) mixing Indian and Oriental references in an exotic, playful and beautiful building. It was a palace by the sea on a grand scale and quite alien compared to its traditional English surroundings.

In the Victorian age of Empire the influence of the Orient, India and also Africa became more acute than ever. As the Victorians moved into an era of mass-produced furniture and textiles, a greater value began to be placed on the hand-crafted fabrics and ceramics of the East – an attitude that lives on today, with widespread respect for the personal touch of the artisan over the tooled precision of factory production. There was also growth of a more ambitious two-way trade, with manufacturers and workshops in India and the East designing and making goods especially for the Western markets. In the West, meanwhile, factories were making their own versions of Oriental and Indian designs, such as Paisley, which Scottish textile manufacturers based on an indigenous Kashmiri pattern.

For the Georgians and particularly the Victorians the integration of wicker work, Japanese screens, blue and white porcelain, Indian cottons or embroidery and other ethnic arts and crafts into their homes was bound up not just with a rose-tinted view of Empire but with ideas of exoticism and romanticism. The nineteenth century was the great age of exploration, of the pioneer adventurers such as Mungo Park, the Scottish explorer who disappeared in 1806 searching for the source of the Niger, of Livingstone and Stanley's famous meeting near the shores of Lake Tanganyika in November, 1871, and of Burton and Speke's terrible journey to find the source of the Nile in the 1850s. It was also the golden era of boyish imperial fiction, such as Rider Haggard's *King Soloman's Mines* (1886), R.M. Ballantyne's *The Gorilla Hunters* (1862) and *Black Ivory* (1873), or Kipling's picaresque stories such as *The Jungle Book* and *Kim*, published around the turn of the century. At the same time, across the Atlantic, Jack London was publishing his own tales of adventure and travel, such as *The Call of the Wild* (1903), *White Fang* (1906) and *South Sea Tales* (1911).

In many ways we are still affected by this romantic, adventurous view of travel which so intrigued and possessed the Victorians. There is also the powerful image of the treasure hunters to be considered and the potent legacy they too have left upon our imaginations.

Figures such as Howard Carter, who opened Tutankhamen's tomb in 1922, or American explorer Hiram Bingham who discovered the Inca city of Machu Picchu in 1911 in the mountains of the Andes, nestling upon terraces overlooking the Urubamba River. And there is the power and the glory of film and television — especially Hollywood — which has seeped into our lives and filtered into our minds, often portraying an idealistic and simplistic picture of other exotic cultures.

The world is, of course, shrinking a little more every single day and is available to us in an unprecedented way. Almost every road has been mapped, the romanticised life of the great explorer all but a dream. Yet we still hold onto this idea of discovery and adventure, although in a more personal sense. What we have today is the possibility of discovering for ourselves, seeing and experiencing places such as Machu Picchu, Lake Tanganyika or the great Indian temples of Madurai or Konarak. And making discoveries of a more intimate kind: foods and spices, sounds and vistas as well as fabrics, paintings and prayer scrolls, a carved Buddha from Thailand, Masai beadwork, Kente cloth in reds and oranges from Ghana, Javanese terracotta, Lao ikats and more. We also bring back discoveries of more important principles which we can apply to the canvases of our homes. Lessons in symmetry and uncluttered living from Japan, for instance, or ideas from the airy homes of Indonesia about utilising open spaces such as terraces and verandahs. Ideas about light and colour from India or of open-plan style from the lofts of Manhattan. But most important of all is the discovery of inspiration, which has to be one of the greatest by-products of modern-day travelling.

How far and how deeply inspiration strikes us, naturally, is a very personal affair. For some it may be as extreme as creating a contemporary version of a Brighton Pavilion, for others it may result in creating a particular room on an Indian, African or Japanese theme. But for most of us inspiration translates into a fusion of influences and ideas, of pieces that catch the eye when travelling and others found in your own town which now offers such a range of design options imported from all corners of the world that it's easier than ever to translate any design concept into reality.

Yet fusion interiors are not about simply throwing together a collection of disparate elements and hoping they will work with one another, nor about creating a pristine museum of treasures. There is, of course, a welcome informality to contemporary interiors and the 'rules' of fusion interiors are fluid and changing.

Yet there has to be a cohesion to a room, a focused design which brings together eclectic, diverse elements in a seamless way. Often the link can be as simple as colour, but texture and pattern also have strong parts to play, and ideas about symmetry, simplicity and scale taken from other cultures can often help in creating a unified and elegant scheme for a room or home.

As we know from Georgian and Victorian Britain, fusion interiors are not new in themselves. What is new is the choice we now have, not only in terms of travel and accessing a world of design, but also in the selection of what is easily available to us for designing and furnishing our homes. The frame of reference is greater than ever and the markets, souks and bazaars of the world are open to us as never before – directly and indirectly – as long as we have the imagination to appreciate the ideas for sale. And as our homes are slowly infiltrated by new technology, by mass-produced utilitarian necessities, we are learning – just as the Victorians did – to place a higher value on true craftsmanship, on beauty, on being able to see and feel the hand of the artisan behind the objects and textiles we take into our homes, encouraging an emotional as well as an aesthetic response.

What is also new is increasing globalisation and the growth of multicultural societies. This means not only that so much is easily available to us, but also that there is an inevitable blurring, merging and hybridization of stylistic influences. Aspects of design from abroad can find their way into our own design vocabulary without us even being aware of it. Chintz, for example, is thought of as typically English yet the origins are Indian, with the word for the ubiquitous flowery printed cotton originally sourced from the Sanskrit word *chitra*, meaning speckled. A commonplace piece of furniture like a futon comes from the East, of course, while we cover our floors in sisal, coir and seagrass with hardly a thought for the origin. And naturally this cross-pollination of styles works in the other direction, with the traditional ways of home living in Japan and India in particular slowly being eroded or enriched by Western mores.

It is ironic, some might say inevitable, that this same process of globalization both increases stylistic choice and yet at the same time destroys much of the indigenous and ethnic diversity that gave birth to that choice in the first place. Traditional cultures and tribal ways of living in Africa, Latin America and India are under intense threat of extinction. While many of us have learned to appreciate the value of other simpler, slower and more spiritual ways of life – as well as the traditional craftsmanship and skills of many indigenous peoples – there seems little to be done to stop these people becoming a side show on the travel trail we all demand to follow and appreciate.

At Andrew Martin inspiration has always come from a rich mix of sources, from all around the globe, from past and present, from indigenous cultures and even lost civilizations.

The value of escapism and discovery, of rich associations with other times and places, has translated into sophisticated, eclectic designs for fabrics and furnishings which are both contemporary and traditional – updating and reinterpreting ethnic motifs or ideas – and blend seamlessly with artefacts, furniture and statuary sourced from the East, from India and the Americas, as well as from Britain and Europe. It's wish-fulfilment and fantasy mixed with a spirit of adventure – looking to an alternative present and to the past to create future elegance, style and comfort.

This book represents some of the most important influences that have played upon Andrew Martin, providing an atlas of design – with details for each interior provided in a sourcebook at the back of the book – along with a subjective view of those parts of the world that have mattered most. It cannot hope to be comprehensive and some generalizations are inevitable. Yet it can claim to look at those cultures that have made the greatest impact upon Andrew Martin and upon contemporary design. And in presenting the places and people that have inspired us, to perhaps inspire you. It is a book, then, dedicated to the idea of escape through association, of style through diversity, of fusion for the home.

Orient

The Orient has always had a vital and intoxicating influence on interior design. China, especially, has played a part in reshaping Western ideas about design for over 400 years, from the days of the Silk Road when Europe began to adopt the beauty and artistry of chinoiserie, lacquerware, silks and porcelain for its great houses. Today, we are just as likely to be inspired by the traditional ikat weaving of Malaysia, the bright colours of Indonesian batik or Thai silk, Indonesian carved teak furniture, terracotta jars and statuary. And Japan, too, has gradually exported a whole philosophy of design based upon cohesive simplicity which has helped to promote the rise of a more ordered style of living and a focused approach to home design, with an emphasis on symmetry and maximizing natural light. There is a powerful diversity and sophistication to Eastern design which continues to fascinate and inspire.

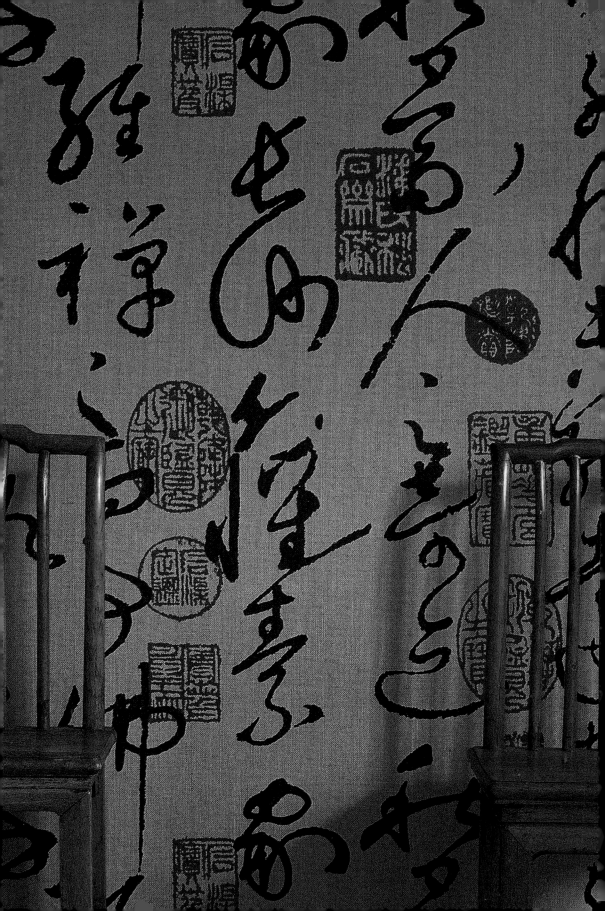

The rich colours and artistry of Oriental craftsmanship stand out upon the canvas of the home.

In China, the line between art and design has long been slim and flexible while the sophistication and sheer quality of its decorative crafts have been widely respected for centuries. Yet along with the intensity of colour in Chinese lacquer, porcelain, celadon or silks, along with its innate fineness, comes a feeling that a little goes a long way. A bold chinoiserie panel or wallpaper design can easily transform a room, a deep red Chinese lacquer cabinet can effortlessly stand out as a centrepiece, a calligraphic pattern for an upholstered chair or sofa can immediately seize and please the eye.

Chinese and Oriental design offers up the idea that less can be more, that there is a need for care in balancing bold colour and patterns with a lighter touch for an interior that strikes an elegant, restrained note.

You must know that it is the greatest palace that ever was. The roof is very lofty and the walls of the palace are all covered with gold and silver. They are also adorned with dragons, beasts and birds, knights and idols. And on the ceiling too you see nothing but gold and silver. The building is altogether so vast, so rich and so beautiful that no man on earth could design anything superior to it.

Marco Polo, on the court of Kublai Khan in Beijing, from *The Book of Ser Marco Polo* (1298).

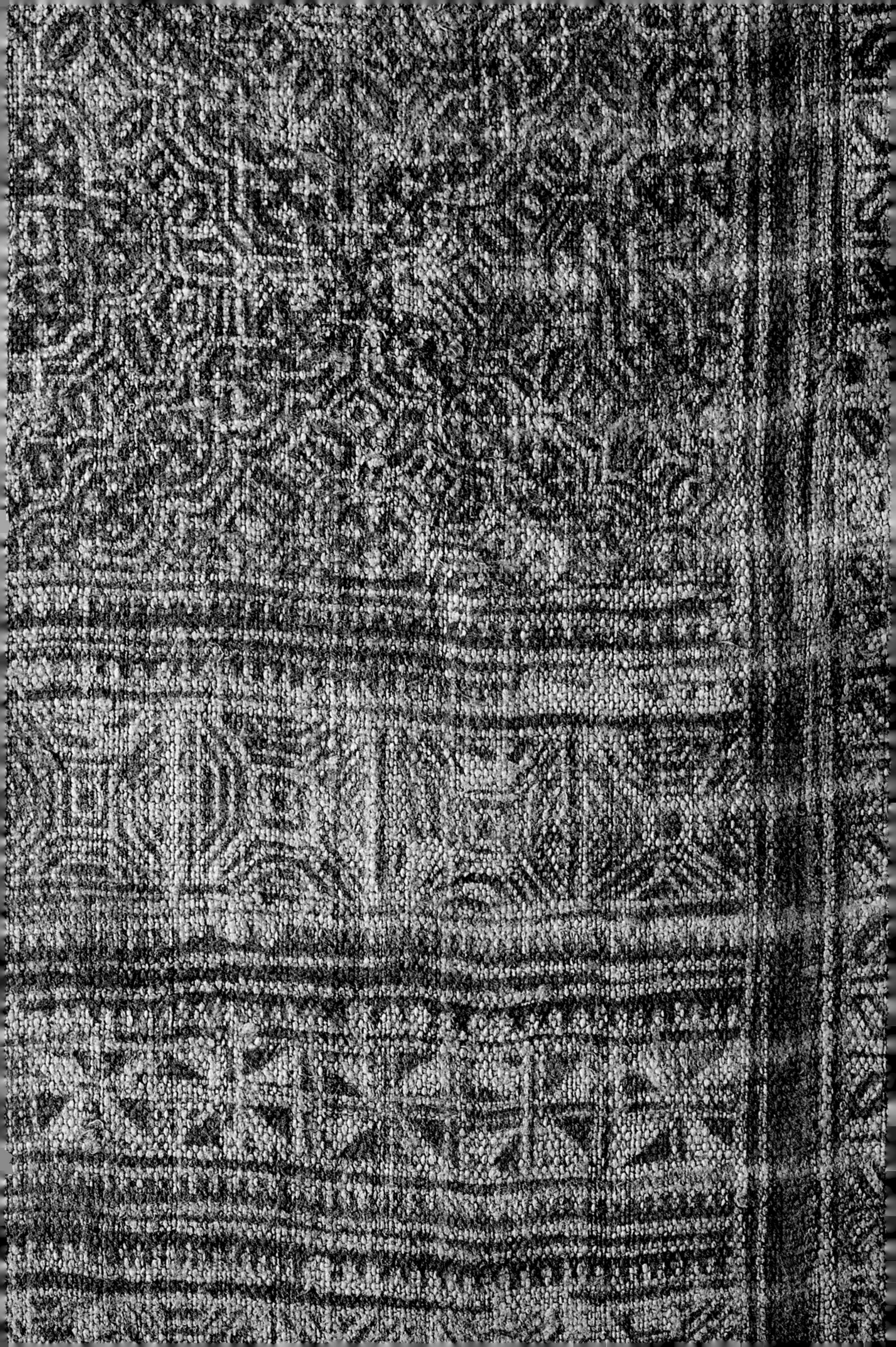

In the world of design the Orient has long been dominated by the brooding, provocative presence of China. There has always been a sense that, historically, China pioneered decorative arts and crafts, which then filtered through to other Far Eastern cultures and were in turn adopted with fascinated enthusiasm by the West.

Imperial China reached a dramatic level of sophistication in its applied arts very early on, continuing to refine and develop its pool of skills as other empires, such as the Roman, Byzantine and Persian empires, rose and then fell away. By the time of Confucius (551–479 BC) China had established a powerful, if disparate, achievement in science, philosophy and design.

There is still a widespread respect for the long, rich history and artistry of Chinese style.

We visit the Terracotta Army of the Emperor Qin at Xi'an, in Shaanxi Province, and look at the rows and ranks of soldiers and horses – originally painted in a dozen or more bright colours, complete with chariots and swords – created to accompany the Emperor into the afterlife. Qin, who ruled in the third century BC, was the First Emperor – the ruler who brought the Chinese empire together on a grand scale and began the long, slow process of unification across an epic landscape. And it was Qin who ordered the construction of the Great Wall, 1,500 miles long from west to east, later rebuilt by the Ming emperors as protection against the Mongol armies.

From the days of Marco Polo, who travelled from Venice to China in the thirteenth century, staying in Peking for sixteen years at the court of Kublai Khan, Western travellers have wondered at the scale of China and the grandeur of its architecture. There is the Grand Canal, built in the early seventh century, stretching for 1,200 miles and one of the most heroic achievements of the Sui and Tang Dynasties, which presided over and encouraged a new age of enlightenment for the arts and design, as well as for architecture, crowned by the great Tang capital of Xi'an. Hundreds of years later it was the Ming emperor Chengzu who was responsible not only for making Beijing the country's new capital, but for creating a revitalized, modern Chinese city, which included the great series of walls and palaces that became the Forbidden City.

To think of silk is to think of China, which harboured the production and manufacture of fine silk as a state secret for centuries and monopolized a trade which gave rise to the ancient Silk Road, winding its way from the Mediterranean coast through Tashkent, Khiva, Bukhara and Samarkland to eastern China. For a period of a thousand years from around 250 BC, the Chinese used bolts of silk as currency. Approximately 2,000 spinning silkworms feeding on the leaves of mulberry trees were needed to produce just one pound of the precious strands.

The Romans under Caesar appreciated and enjoyed Chinese silk, the treasured fabrics finding their way far into the Roman empire through relays of merchant traders and exchanged for gold or horses.

Both Japanese silk and the slightly rougher Thai silk owe their origins to answers and ideas originally passed on by the Chinese artisans.

And the same can be said of other fine disciplines, such as porcelain, celadon and lacquerware which gradually filtered out to other Asian territories such as Japan, Korea, Thailand and Burma.

There is a long tradition of perfecting fine and exquisite glazes and finishes, detailed designs and patterns in paper-thin porcelain. Collectors across the world place unquestioning value on the quality of Chinese porcelain and look back to the Ming dynasty of the fourteenth to eighteenth centuries, especially, as a golden age for Oriental ceramics. Imperial patronage led to the supremacy of the kilns of the Jiangxi province town of Jingdezhen, the quality of its porcelain so fine that ceramics were often deliberately shattered by their makers if the work failed tests of colour or form. Artisans employed in the factories would concentrate on just one aspect, such as moulding, glazing or firing, and each piece might pass through ten or more pairs of hands.

Jingdezhen blue and white porcelain was especially admired, with growing orders from the West meeting any trading shortfalls when imperial demand started to seep away in the seventeenth century.

The colours of the glazes were so intense that three hundred years later, pieces of Ming china found on the bed of the South China Sea, by the wrecks of trade clippers, still have an unmistakable sheen and richness.

From the sixteenth and seventeenth centuries, a strong and regular trade with Europe developed and demand rose in the West not only for porcelain and precious silks but for the luxurious, exotic finery of lacquer, Chinese painting and the almost unparalleled quality of Chinese carpets. Chinese designs began to have a permanent place in European homes and the touch of Oriental craftsmanship, including hand-painted Chinese wallpapers and delicate chinoiserie panelling, can be still seen in most great English country houses, such as Nostell Priory in Yorkshire, Saltram near Plymouth and Claydon House in Buckinghamshire, dating from the seventeenth to nineteenth centuries.

The influence of Chinese design became ingrained in the minds and styles of Western architects, such as John Nash and William Chambers.

And designers, including Thomas Chippendale, adopted and adapted chinoiserie alongside Gothic, neo-classical and Louis XVI styles. Elements like chinoiserie became so much a part of English and other European style book references that they have become familiar to the point where they barely register as exotic. The Victorians sometimes took their fascination with the Orient to the point of obsession. The refined and formal quality of Chinese design fitted in well with the Victorian home aesthetic, as it had done earlier for the Georgians. It was sympathetically and successfully applied on the smaller scale of the Victorian terraced house. Tortoiseshell and lacquered screens, ivory and porcelain, Chinese cabinets and silk wall hangings – all were taken up by the Victorians with a passion.

There is a permanence to the influence of Chinese architecture, art and design and its slow integration into Western design and home style. The impact of Oriental and imperial colours, for instance, is profound.

These are predominantly imperial tones associated with wealth, power and drama. They are so familiar to us now that paint charts adopt the country as an adjective in itself: 'China Red', 'Chinese Yellow', 'Imperial Green'.

The lavish reds of China have a special resonance – the colour of imperial seals, of shining silks. Chinese lacquerware gleams in polished reds, found upon

Chinese cabinets, screens, tables and trays. Countless shades of red sit naturally in the context of Oriental design, from the duller tones of terracotta to the recessive, dark ink reds found in Chinese calligraphy. These deep, rich colours bring real intimacy and fiery warmth to any room. Strong emerald greens come with a sheen that has become popular in tile glazes where there is a desire for a luxurious colour with an intense, opulent depth. These are vibrant colours with a bold, solid effect, although in the glazes of celadon ceramics we find a more translucent quality, almost like coloured glass, in light greens, greys and blues, yet still rich and shining and quite contemporary in its simplicity.

Calligraphic patterns in shades of scarlet and vermilion add drama in wallpapers and fabrics, while richly coloured table runners and wall banners add an almost effortless splash of fine, exuberant colour to a dining room. And with furniture, there is a beauty in the patina of age that flatters antique pieces, as they tend to mix more naturally into the home without dominating the space they inhabit. Even when ancient and distressed – as with antique, double-doored wedding cabinets, now

commonly seen in Western homes – the tantalizing message of colour seeps gently through.

In Japan, black has a wider currency than crimson or even jade. Polished black lacquerware has now been reinvented as a modern finish for contemporary furniture, although its origins are ancient.

Lacquer comes from tree sap, which begins to turn black and harden when drained from the living plant. The sap is mixed into a paste and applied in layers to a delicate framework of bamboo or wood and then carefully dried. The many layers are polished and smoothed to produce a rich gloss, while coloured pigments can be added to the lacquer paste to achieve different shades or the possibility of etching intricate patterns into the lacquer to a base colour below. It is black lacquer that Japan is best known for, now made into sleek shapes for tables, plates, bowls and vases. And black has a value in interiors as a true source of drama, adding a basic shock to a dull room.

White, too, has a special place in Japanese design, almost alien to the

Chinese who associate white with death. It's the translucent white of rice paper, used in shoji screens and sliding panels, or the simple white of fine, virgin china and of ivory. It's a white that breaks down hard, solid divisions in the home in favour of a more integrated, lightly partitioned space which allows light to filter through a house while still offering the sense of privacy and formality so prized in Japanese interiors. And tones of white tend to be associated with modern materials, such as polished concrete and stone, glazed white ceramic tiles and white painted walls, now bound up with very modern ideas about Zen minimalism.

Certainly there is a temptation to think of the cultivated simplicity of Japanese interiors in terms of a principally modern aesthetic, **partly because Japan has reinvented itself over the past fifty years as such a progressive, modern society with a matching architecture and technology.**

Yet the refined minimalist Modernism of Japanese designers and architects such as Tadao Ando, Kenzo Tange and Kisho Kurokawa fits naturally with the long evolution of traditional Japanese style.

There has always been a formality to Japanese homes together with an emphasis on symmetry and straight lines, ceremony, restraint and order.

In traditional Japanese interiors there is relatively little in the way of free-standing furniture. The floor is furnished with cushions, mattresses, futons and low lying tables and used as a place for sitting, eating, relaxing and sleeping. The clutter of everyday life tends to be stored away and a great emphasis is placed on ritual – in eating, bathing, receiving guests, taking tea. But there is also a real sense of style mixed with utility, with the use of semi-opaque screens, light wells and sliding fusuma paper-covered doors making the most of all available space and sunlight.

In many ways the minimalism of Japanese interior style seems at odds with the fuller, more expressive eclecticism and luxury of fusion interiors. Yet there is value in looking and learning from elements of Japanese home style, especially in regard to restraint. There is always the temptation in the home to surround oneself with anything that takes the eye, anything that captures the imagination. The result can often be a crowded room where nothing can breathe, while the intrinsic beauty of the things that matter to you is suffocated. From Japan comes the idea that there is sense in restraint, that it can allow you to really savour and enjoy a painting, a fabric, a texture, a splash of colour.

'Nothing is more striking in a Japanese room than the harmonies and contrasts between the colours of the various objects and the room itself', said Victorian commentator Edward Morse in the 1880s, writing in his book *Japanese Homes and their Surroundings*, which describes Japanese style in very similar terms to the way we still think today. 'The general tone of the room sets off to perfection the simplest spray of flowers, a quiet picture, a rough bit of pottery or an old bronze; and at the same time a costly and magnificent piece of gold lacquer blazes out like a gem from these simple surroundings – and yet the harmony is not disturbed.'

Without going to the impersonal, antiseptic extremes of minimalism, one can also see with Japanese interiors how much drama this harmonious, neutral backdrop can add to a room where the colours and patterns of fabrics can stand out with prominence. It allows a concentration on a more subtle use of texture, with a spectrum of natural tones for bamboo blinds, sisal flooring or the tatami reed mats common to many Japanese homes, neutral cottons or linens, stone statuary and a reserved use of colour.

As with China, the West has long looked to Japan for inspiration of one kind or another.

In the nineteenth century, as the fast-growing Victorian middle classes enthused about the Oriental look, there was a great demand for Japanese woodcuts, ceramics and for lacquer, largely known to the Victorians as japanning. Towards the end of the nineteenth century Arthur Lasenby Liberty founded Liberty & Company and began importing decorative artwork from Japan, China and India. Japanese furniture reached new heights of glamour and fashion with screens, for instance, used as room dividers, just as they are increasingly being used again in contemporary interiors.

This passion for hand-crafted Japanese and Chinese design was in part a reaction to the mass production of European manufacturers, busy turning out standardized designs. Among Arts and Crafts designers, who turned their backs upon mechanized manufacturing in favour of the hand-crafted work of the true artisan, there was something of a natural affinity with the innate skill of Oriental and Japanese designers, with figures such as William Morris and Charles Voysey introducing exotic motifs and patterns – many of them incorporating familiar references to birds, blossoms and twisting creepers – into wallpapers and textiles partly inspired by Oriental models.

The appeal of Japanese design then and now is to do with detail.

There is a crafted precision to Japanese style, an attention to finishes, line and form which offers general inspiration in favour of care. As the maxim says, 'God is always in the detail', and this remains true even in the context of both fusion style and of the growing informality of Western contemporary interior design.

This trend towards informality suits the indulgent nature of fusion design. The taste for a more relaxed, comfortable look has coincided with a surge of interest in South-East Asia, in the arts and crafts of Thailand, Indonesia and Malaysia. These countries, with others –

Cambodia and Vietnam especially – have become increasingly popular as travel destinations, gradually growing in stature and accessibility.

While China and Japan have always had a formality and refinement to their decorative arts – which from the seventeenth century onwards suited the mannered qualities of European interiors and architecture – South-East Asia has exhibited a more rustic approach to design. Whereas Japan and China developed a complex system of patronage and apprenticeship which encouraged the progression of the decorative arts, architecture and design, other parts of Asia developed a more organic, peasant-based artistry. Instead of silk weavers working in imperial factories, we think of Indonesian ikat weavers labouring by their wooden, stilt-raised homes.

Instead of building up a great export trade like China, South-East Asian artisans principally made for the domestic market, for their own homes or those of their neighbours.

This provides an occasionally idealistic element of authenticity to the crafts of

Java, Bali or Vietnam. Yet certainly it is more ethnic, in the way we tend to imagine ethnic design, and much of it evolved from the necessity of creating basic, everyday objects. In more recent years Western travellers and buyers have learned to place a greater value than ever upon this kind of craftsmanship, seeing within it the hand and touch of the maker, perhaps the quality of indigenous cultural expression. It has helped provoke a shift in the way we think of design, seeing that there is a charm in imperfection, that an antique does not have to be perfect and finely finished, but can have far more interest and character if it is worn with use and distressed by time.

The true history of the development of Asian craftsmanship might well be a little more complex, bearing in mind the way Chinese artisans spread their method and message through the region. Celadon ceramics are Chinese in origin, for instance, although now common not only to Japan but also Korea and Thailand. Contemporary lacquerware, often Westernized to demand in function and form yet still sleek and beautiful, is now as likely to be from Vietnam or Burma as from China or Japan. Lacquerware was introduced into South-East Asia by the Chinese as early as the first century AD and Burma is said to have the largest lacquer industry in the East, dating back to around the eleventh century.

The production of Thai silk, too, has its origins in China but was taken up with enthusiasm and skill early in Thailand's history and by the seventeenth century was being exported as an alternative to Chinese silk.

Although rather coarser than the Chinese equivalent, Thai silk now has a great popularity after being commercially revived in the 1940s and 1950s, largely by American architect and designer Jim Thompson. Thompson introduced colour-fast dyeing techniques, commercial looms and a wider choice of colours, his version of Thai silks achieving a new level of fame when they were featured in stage and screen productions of *The King and I*. The silk company Thompson, founded in Bangkok, is still very much part of the interior design establishment, with its heavier silks now also used for upholstery. Often seen in a bolder spectrum of colours and patterns, such as the checks common to traditional

Thai menswear, Thai silks can be more vivid and luminous than Chinese versions, with a textural quality born of raised imperfections in the weave.

But other textiles are seen as truly indigenous to South-East Asia. Ikats, from the Malaysian word for binding, were traditionally produced over the course of many weeks with the yarn tied and dyed before weaving and then painstakingly made up into elaborate, complex patterns. The use of natural dyes on cotton, linen and sometimes silk meant that the colour range used to be one of reds, oranges, yellows, indigo and deep reds to black. Now ikats, which are found across the entire region, from Indonesia to Thailand, are seen in a whole range of colours and fibres, many of them brighter and more artificial in their range of tones. With images of birds, horses, deer and elephants, as well as more abstract designs, ikats were often associated with rituals such as marriage and funerals but now have a wide popularity as wall hangings, throws or rugs in thicker weaves, as well as being used as curtains and table runners.

Batik is thought to have authentic Indonesian roots. From a Javanese word for painted, batik was first made with Indian cotton traded for spices. Molten wax is painted onto the cotton in patterns, and when the fabric is dipped into dye, the wax design resists the colour. The process is repeated many times to create a complicated, intricate and multi-coloured textile. Centred upon Indonesia, especially Java, batik still has the power to impress with its sophistication and rich use of colour, even though it is now produced on a larger scale and more commercial basis. Classic Oriental motifs – such as dragons, peacocks, butterflies, creepers and vines – contrast with more abstract designs in rich red, indigo and russet colours.

Across Indonesia there is a contrast between the more rustic style typical of village workshops and a refined, elaborate Javanese style characterized by detailed carving with richly grained wood.

Teak is widely used and traditional carved cabinets and four-poster beds – open to one side, bordered by carved miniature balustrading on the other three edges – are particularly fine. Traditional, low Indonesian beds are often converted to sofas for the Western market.

Across the Orient there has always been a tendency towards floor living: sitting on the floor to eat, talk and entertain.

In Thai furniture this same traditional orientation towards the floor can be seen in beds, sofas, chairs and tables, along with an occasional Chinese influence in the use of very intricate lacquered patterning or fine carving. As well as the production of more modern, Westernized furniture, original Thai pieces have often been converted to Western use: altar tables become console tables, preaching chairs become domestic armchairs.

This adaptation of traditional ethnic designs to a more decorative use is wrapped up in the whole idea of fusion interiors. Basket-weaving, for example, developed across Indonesia and elsewhere in Asia mostly in response to a need for storing rice and other foods. Now basketry from Borneo, Sarawak, Thailand and Java is used in Western homes – along with woven fish traps, Javanese and Thai terracotta – adding texture, colour and interest to a room.

Artefacts such as carved, lacquered or bronze Buddhas, rich with age, have a wonderful decorative impact in the home beyond their original religious importance in the sacred spaces of Oriental homes and places of worship. Some of that same intrinsic appeal might be found in many everyday objects, such as large, glazed water jars, a pair of embroidered slippers or bamboo trays. Ironically, across much of Asia the attitude is that new is best, that lacquer should be flawless, a golden Buddha is far better if untainted and undamaged, and antiques are seldom accorded the same sense of value as in the West.

Yet we have adopted some South-East Asian attitudes, such as the familiar way Japanese and Chinese homes try to integrate the outside and inside. This has become very important in modern Western architecture, with a growing realization that verandahs and decks, courtyards and terraces, can increase the feeling of space and light, adding to the look and feel of interconnecting, enclosed interior spaces.

Asian homes also tend towards a contrast between dark rooms and light spaces, offering the choice – according to the level of heat – to retreat or take advantage of the breeze and sunlight.

Again, this is an idea to consider for any home in terms of providing contrasts and creating varied atmospheres to suit dining, relaxing and cooking. Colour and light always affect the mood of a room, and spaces for indulgence often suit a darker, more intimate treatment in warmer shades and fabrics. Even the Oriental principle that furniture should be at the centre of a room, not pushed to the sides as we have tended to do in the West, has helped to re-evaluate and enrich attitudes to the home.

There is a huge diversity within what we broadly label an 'Oriental' look – a great resource of colours, textures, objects, fabrics and patterns to draw upon. And with an often overlapping heritage in terms of craftsmanship, materials, motifs and finishes, there is this reassurance that Indonesian will usually sit well with Chinese, Chinese with Japanese and so on, as long as there are common threads to a room in terms of colour or texture. And beyond that, there are many other possibilities for a fusion of eclectic styles.

The more rustic, unpolished elements of South-East Asian style sit well with a heritage look (see pages 246–82), which looks back to a pre-Renaissance European legacy of design with a rougher, unpolished, semi-primitive edge to it. Japanese style, too, is enjoying such interest partly because there is a sense of modernity to the whole Japanese attitude to home style, even though it is deeply rooted in tradition. The elegant simplicity and restraint of Japanese style not only suits more contemporary spaces but can act as a bridge between a more modern home and the introduction of traditional aspects of Chinese design, as well as the more rustic flavours of Indonesia, introducing an important element of warm, luxurious exoticism.

Whatever the mix of ethnic and contemporary, polished finishes and rougher textures, the point of restraint should stay in the mind within the creation of a total, cohesive look based on principles of colour co-ordination, textural contrasts and sheer comfort.

In interior design it is always best to move towards this mixture, this rich union of influences, rather than opt for a simplistic and easy statement. Because a room must have interest, escapism and many separate stories. This is the ideal of fusion interiors.

From the Introduction

A Ndebele woman of Zimbabwe wearing traditional brass neck rings or dzilla.

A Masai woman adorned with brightly coloured beadwork.

Mountaineers ascending a glacial pinnacle of ice – or serac – in the 1890s.

Camels wind their way across a Mongolian desert plain during a Trans-Asiatic expedition by the American Museum of Natural History in 1925.

Ranks of elephants carry their passengers across the river at Perak, Malaysia, in the last years of the nineteenth century.

A Peru-Bolivian Boundary Commission expedition sails the waters of the River Manuripe in Peru, 1911, surrounded by tangled greenery.

Exploring rock formations among the foothills of the Andes in the border country between Peru and Bolivia in 1911.

From Orient

A group of llamas – the monks and priests of Tibetan and Mongolian Buddhism in traditional costume – captured on film in the Himalayas, 1894.

The distinctive wing shapes of projecting eaves characterise the elaborate roofline of a Chinese temple designed in the form of inter-connecting towers three or four storeys high.

In China calligraphy became established as a fine art, with the skill of master practitioners revered and emulated. Here the word Shanghai is written in calligraphy characters.

An anonymous Chinese man striking a pose for the camera at his home in Sinkiang in the 1870s, complete with bamboo table, patterned rug and traditional dress.

Japanese silk and textile traders presenting their goods in the 1870s surrounded by patterned hanging curtains.

Shoppers and their children make their way down a dusty Shanghai trading street in 1906.

Calligraphy brushes of all sizes hang in a shop. The wide choice of brush and inks suggests the complexity and high-ranking status of the craft.

Chinese rice farmers in raincoats and traditional peaked bamboo-straw hats plant seedlings in paddy fields at Guizhou Sheng.

Farm labourers use bullocks to plough paddy fields in the early years of the twentieth century.

Safari

In Africa everything comes back

to landscape, to nature. This is especially true of colours and textures, along with a simpler way of living bound up with the imposed, romantic ideal of safari. All emerge, one way or another, from the landscape – vast, different and full of stories. Yet Africa is also about what has been lost, or is very much under threat, it is about past empires and disappearing tribes. And with them they take parts of a culture and a way of life that over centuries has given rise to such a rich and ethnic tapestry of design. Just as they fight for their future, we are recognizing and becoming intrigued by the beauty of a simpler, more organic form of design that mostly springs out of utility and spiritual rituals, expressions of belief. Yet it is also an epic and exotic continent of unimaginable variety. Look to the north and you see a very different Africa, shaped by Islam, and a more solid expression of a great architectural heritage as strong and alive as any comparisons to be made with homelands across the warm waters of the Mediterranean.

Much of the strength of African design emerges through the constant vibrancy of texture.

Across the sub-Saharan continent, texture comes in all its forms: the worked suedes or harder leathers that come from animal hides of every kind; the miniature cobblestone effect of brightly coloured beadwork; the raw, unpolished state of wooden carvings from masks to tribal sculptures. And then there is the textural appeal of natural fibres such as jute, sisal, seagrass and coir – used more commonly in contemporary interiors than ever before – as well as banana fibre, papyrus and sorghum for woven baskets. Add to that the rough, beaten metals of African jewellery in copper, brass and ironwork. The value of texture shines through in the neutral shades associated with Africa – sand, ochre, tan and many shades of red and brown. The impact of texture should never be undervalued in the home, where it provokes a response from the senses and adds layers of interest and beauty. Eclectic elements and symbols of safari fantasy also seep back into our living rooms to tempt our imaginations: old traveller's trunks, hunting trophies, leopard-skins, fading maps, old tribal shields and sepia photographs.

Texture and pattern play the most important roles in the amalgamation of traditional African designs into the palette of fusion style.

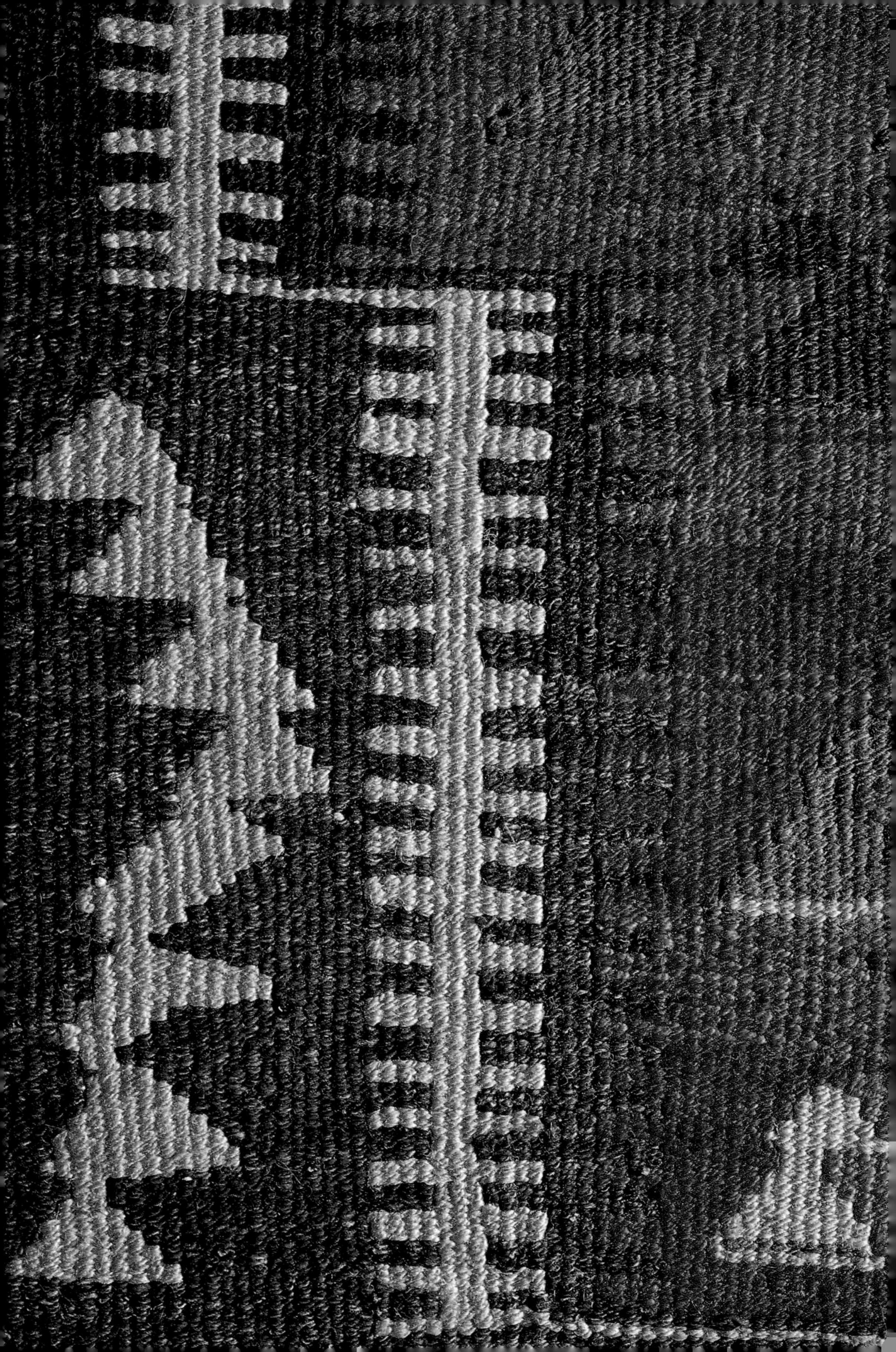

In our minds we tend to either over-romanticize Africa or think of it bleakly as a dark, lost continent, while all the time reality treads the ground in between. The great Victorian explorers, such as David Livingstone, Richard Burton, John Hanning Speke or Sir Samuel White Baker, were only at the start of a long and ongoing process of Westerners realizing the rich diversity and history of Africa. Constantly searching for something new, there was a high price to pay for their explorations: Mungo Park drowned seeking the source of the Niger; James Bruce took himself through 'numberless dangers and sufferings' in his quest for the source of the Nile, the same terrible venture that later ate the friendship and spirit of Burton and Speke. Yet the true source for understanding Africa, as with any country, lies with the people themselves.

Africa, like the Orient, experienced many golden ages and empires before it ever suffered the attention of other imperial powers from overseas. The monumental stone city of Great Zimbabwe, for instance, was built around the eleventh or twelfth century by the Shona people. It was the capital of a sophisticated trading state, rich in gold and ivory, but then abandoned in the sixteenth century. The Ashanti empire, centred upon modern-day Ghana, was at its height around the seventeenth century after hundreds of years of ascendancy, becoming a wealthy trade power. And in Mali, the cities of Timbuktu and Djenne were important cultural and political centres throughout the Middle Ages while the many trade routes that crisscross the Sahara are thought to be as much as 5,000 years old.

Yet the great tribes who created such a unique approach to arts and crafts, born of their cultural and spiritual values, are now under threat as never before.

The threat provokes us to look more carefully, more sympathetically at Africa and its heritage. We look with fascination at the colours, patterns and textures of tribal textiles, sculptures and other decorative crafts, with the feeling that they are indicative of a more organic, natural and sensual approach.

The interest in indigenous African design is broader than ever, and increasingly fashionable.

It may be true that we are often tempted to create simplistic associations, but that's not to deny their power. We do think of the great explorers and the exotic imagery of safari – famously idealised in the 1930s by Ernest Hemingway in *The Green Hills of Africa* – and although the camera may have replaced the gun, the whole romantic quality of safari remains alive. We increasingly travel to Africa and come away inspired by what we see.

Our perceptions of other cultures, often romanticized and filtered through film and fiction, are just as important to us as reality and partly shape our approach to design. Part of the reason for the growing fashion for African tribal-inspired design has to do with this rose-tinted view and the associations it brings.

Yet its popularity has a lot to do with a broader reaction against the formality and finery of European interiors which has resulted in a far greater interest in ethnic styles, patterns and colours. We can see this in the growing popularity of South-East Asian arts and crafts.

The use of animal hides, especially, has become an important story in contemporary interiors, partly born of the African influence. The zebra- and leopard-skins of the safari look – faked for the homes of today – are periodically popular, while the increasing use of leather and suede for upholstery has a more enduring magnetism, especially on progressive designs for sofas, ottomans and armchairs. The look of hides such as ocelot, rhino and crocodile, available in convincing imitations, has an even more glamorous appeal.

The growth of interest in natural floorings, such as coir and seagrass, also has many African associations. The neutral tones and wonderful textures of plant fibres for matting and carpets can form a perfect foundation to a room. The desirable neutrality of these materials means that any use of colour in fabrics and paintwork will stand out all the more.

The origins of these floorings lie in basic woven matting and in basket making and the choice of weaves and tones is now broad without losing the appeal of texture and simplicity. Coir is made from coconut husk, soaked and softened so that it can be easily woven, while sisal comes from the fibres of a subtropical bush plant. Jute comes from a plant originally native to India, it is a soft fibre and one of the least hard-wearing, while seagrass is grown in paddy fields and is among the most stain-resistant.

Many of these natural floor coverings are easily marked so should be used with care in kitchens, bathrooms and hallways, but they work well in living rooms or bedrooms, even as floor runners or matting rather than wall to wall carpets. Their natural quality has been so admired that their colours and textures have been replicated in other textiles, such as wool which provides a softer feel underfoot.

Finer weaves of natural fibres, such as raffia, can be used for textured wall coverings, which again offer the idea of a subtle base to build upon with layers of colours and finishes. And given their organic quality, natural fibres fit perfectly with elements from many ethnically inspired looks – Oriental, Latin American, Indian – and blend easily with other natural materials, such as bamboo and wood in all its forms and finishes.

Bare wooden floorboards, too, with their grain and glow, are always effective and can be painted, varnished, ebonised or stained. Again, it is the simplicity and versatility of wood which makes it so suitable as a foundation for the look of a room, whether in modern spaces like industrial lofts or an Edwardian terraced house. As a material, it is timeless.

In much of Africa, unlike in China or Japan, you expect to see wood used in a very rustic, masculine way – unpolished and raw.

The design of the game lodge, for instance, usually relies on a framework of wood in every sense: wooden floors and walls, wood or thatch for the roof and relatively simple wooden beds, desk chairs, and refectory-style dining tables as well as wicker and cane furniture. This same reliance upon crafted wood – a traditional building block for sub-Saharan Africa – can be found in many indigenous homes.

Wood carving, too, is one of the great tribal skills, tied up with ritual associations. African masks have an exotic fascination and lend a much-loved sense of drama to fusion style which stretches far beyond their original purpose, rather like an Oriental carved Buddha or an Indian Hindu icon in bronze or stone. Highly stylized and representational, African masks have an innate power that comes from their ceremonial use. The Dogon people of Mali, for example, are known for the design of their large, severe, T-shaped wooden masks in white and black, adorned with coloured raffia, and used in enacting stories from tribal history. Dancers of the Ivory Coast wear brightly painted masks decorated with feathers and animal hair.

Much African carved statuary also carries ritual connotations. For instance, the carved fertility figures of the Congo basin depict pregnant women. And among the Yoruba people of Nigeria, where there is an especially high proportion of twins, a wooden figure is made should one twin die to commemorate the lost child, offer a shelter for its soul and act as a kind of surrogate for the living twin. The meaning behind such objects makes them all the more evocative and even within more commercial carving – such as the woodwork produced by the Kamba people of Kenya – there is this attractive strand of mysticism.

The same might be said of other crafts, such as metalwork or beadwork. Gold has been associated with Africa – think of the mythical King Solomon's mines, supposedly somewhere in Zimbabwe. Yet even among peoples known for working with gold, such as the Ashanti of Ghana or the Baoule of the Ivory Coast, it is only associated with rank and royalty. Elsewhere, in countries such as Benin, bronze is familiar but iron was most commonly used for jewellery and ornament, with iron bars widely used as currency in the eighteenth century. The nomadic Himba people of Namibia use metal beads of iron in their jewellery, studded into leather for armlets, straps and necklaces. Brass jewellery is widespread among the Wodaabe of Niger and among the Masai, while the Ndebele women of Zimbabwe and South Africa are known for the brass coils, called dzilla, which they wear layered around their elongated necks – a traditional symbol of beauty.

Beadwork is a more recent craft, the delicate glass and porcelain beads used in its making introduced from Europe in the nineteenth century. Yet we think of it as an essentially African art, as it is in its method and perfection. In Western Africa, as with the Yoruba of Nigeria, beadwork is usually worn only by a ruling elite but has a much more democratic and widespread popularity to the East and South. The Masai and Samburu peoples of Kenya use beadwork as an everyday adornment, using rich colours such as reds, blues, greens and yellows. The beads have a simple language to them, the beaded necklaces, belts and headpieces suggesting status and wealth.

The Ndebele and Zulus of South Africa use beadwork on skirts and blankets in geometric designs, striking in their beauty, colour and careful craftsmanship.

And it is through pattern that ethnic African design is now really making its presence felt in contemporary Western interior design. Decorative tribal patterns have ancient origins. You still see the use of pattern in body painting associated with religious and spiritual rituals. The Karo people of Ethiopia – one of Africa's most threatened tribal cultures – paint their entire bodies in white and overlay a vivid red sequence of red dots, while Karo women commonly use scarification to create patterns on the surface of the skin. In Sudan, the Nuba cover themselves in ochre or ash and then trace patterns in this coat of colour. Elsewhere, the Ndebele place a great emphasis on the importance of wall painting, tracing complex geometric patterns on the exterior plaster walls of their homes.

In textiles the simple patterns of Mali mud cloth – incorporating diamond motifs and zigzag lines, dots and dashes – are now much imitated and commercially reproduced. Originally made by the Bamana people, the fabric was dyed with river mud creating a deep brown geometric pattern on heavy cream cotton, with the symbolism of the motifs creating a message within the design suited to its ceremonial or commemorative purpose. The same can be said of Kente cloth made by the Ashanti in Ghana, again much copied and commercialized. The colours of Kente cloth are richer, the fabric densely woven, with bold stripes of reds, oranges and yellows. With its roots dating back at least four centuries, the cloth was originally worn as a mark of status, like Ashanti-crafted gold, and each pattern is designed to represent a quality such as courage or strength.

African woven fabrics have a 5,000-year history and there is a wealth of difference among African textile design.

The informed ideal that there is hidden meaning deep within adds an extra dimension to the aesthetic quality of the cloth. Adinkara, another Ashanti fabric, uses a complex variety of symbols and motifs which can be read like a text. In the rich earth colours and symmetrical designs of Kasai velvet from the Congo – made from cut and tufted raffia – we also look for veins of symbolism. Even in mass-produced cotton kangas or sarongs – copies of Masai or Samburu designs – we feel that perhaps there is a hidden depth to the design.

Far to the north, on the other side of the Sahara, there is the influence of Berber textiles from the Maghreb in rich reds and blues, contrasting with sandy base tones. The designs are often simpler than many other African tribal designs and certainly less elaborate than multicoloured Persian kilims. There is an effective clarity and confident use of strong colour in Berber designs, not dissimilar in some ways to Latin American indigenous textiles. One Moroccan tribe – the Tuareg – are known as the 'blue men' because of the way indigo stains their skins as they dye cloth and wool. Walk through the souks of Marrakesh and you see dyed bundles of wool hanging outside dye shops in the richest reds, yellows and oranges that find their way into the symmetrical designs of many kilims.

Yet in many ways the design culture of North Africa with its Islamic opulance seems a world away from the rest of the African continent across the Sahara.

As well as the strong Islamic culture throughout the Maghreb and the legacy of a once-energetic Moorish empire, the proximity to Europe has also meant a long history of trade with other Mediterranean countries and the wealth and seeping influences which that brings. At the same time, Morocco, especially, continues to make a strong impression on the minds and styles of many European designers.

The architecture of the Maghreb, too, has played an important role inspiring ideas in Western contemporary design. The fashion for mosaics can be traced, in part, to the wide use of tiles – or zelliges – in traditional architecture. There has been the powerful influence of more traditional finishes such as tadelakt – a stucco-like treatment for walls or floors, made of sand and quicklime which is then highly polished with soap and stone for a subtle sheen – as well as the impression made by the artistry of Arabesque decorative paintwork and ironwork.

Local African architects and designers are now looking to revitalize the interest in traditional building methods and design, realizing that there can be a quality of fresh modernity to the simple use of methods such as tadelakt or pisé (the traditional Berber adobe material of sun-dried earth with added quicklime and straw). The organic, curving cohesion of a smooth tadelakt shower bath arising from the floor of a bathroom, or a tadelakt fireplace arching out effortlessly from a wall without a broken line, are achievements in integrated style which many contemporary Western architects are also working to achieve. In grander riad town houses, where every room leads off a central courtyard and there's hardly a need for a solid internal door, the principles of open living also fascinate Western designers, together with some of the architectural ideas partly inspired by Islamic culture: horseshoe and keyhole arches for windows or doorways, corner fireplaces as opposed to centred mantles, and wet rooms modelled upon the hammam.

The mix of organic modernity, ethnic simplicity and Islamic sophistication creates a flexibility to North African style which partly explains its wide influence upon contemporary interior designers.

Its more cultivated elements – ceramics, mosaics, polished tadelakt finishes – sit very well with the more refined aspects of Japanese and Chinese style, as well as fusing neatly into modern spaces alongside synthetic materials.

There is also a perfect ingredient of flexibility to elements such as suede, leather and other hides, which have strong African associations. These work as coverings for almost any design of furniture, from modern Italian to traditional English. The fluid textural qualities of natural fibres also transcend practically any look or design scheme and can promise to provide an elegant, neutral base for experimenting further with colour and texture.

Berber patterns, kilims, Moroccan ironwork and glass tie in well to the more rustic appeal of South-East Asian style and Latin American influences.

Tribal patterns, meanwhile, demand a lighter touch, although they can be relied upon to create instant interest and are usually effective in moderation as throws or cushion coverings. And the rich associations inherent in tribal arts and crafts – masks, jewellery, basketry – create an instant sense of drama when used as decorative focal points.

Sunset over a waterhole at Nata in north Botswana.

Archaeologist Dr Alfred Percival Mardsley – travelling light with trestle table, hammock and folding chair – making notes on a field trip in 1889.

A Masai warrior from the village of Olonana in Kenya with an ostrich feather headdress – a traditional symbol of bravery.

A carved wooden dance shield, intricately decorated in a zigzag pattern, from the Kikuyu people of Kenya.

The geometric patterns of this painted wall of a home in Sirigu, Ghana represent people joining hands

Rock engravings of giraffes, rhinos and other animals at Twyfelfontein in Namibia.

The organic simplicity of the rising wood and dried mud towers of a mosque at Mopti in Mali, Western Africa, near the River Niger.

The Samburu people of Kenya use ornate necklaces and facial ornaments as part of the rituals of everyday life. The brightly coloured beads – as worn by this Samburu girl – are often used to suggest status and wealth.

A trader leads his camel to the wood market at Keren in Eritrea, Eastern Africa.

A salt caravan makes its way across the Taodenni plane in northern Mali, leading towards Timbuktu.

Wooden doors in a mud and straw gateway – simply decorated with needle-like motifs – at the mosque at Mopti, Mali.

These severe, rectangular masks decorated with geometric patterns are used by the Dogon people of Mali in enacting out scenes from tribal history.

Village girls, working by mud huts topped with conical straw roofs, use a pestle and mortar to grind maize at Syoma in Mali.

A Turgata young woman with beadwork necklaces, bangles and metal earrings in the Sugata Valley, northern Kenya.

Masai warriors, women and children – dressed in bright traditional dress and beadwork necklaces – sing and dance at a female initiation ceremony in northern Tanzania.

The undulating sands of the Namib desert, Namibia.

Inca

The Incas offer the perfect example

of a proud, lost culture. It seems almost unbelievable even now to imagine the existence of such a powerful, sophisticated empire. Coming into being in the eleventh and twelfth centuries, it flourished right up until the sixteenth century when the Spanish conquistadors destroyed the Inca civilization in just a matter of years. Inca towns and cities were looted for the promise of gold, the Inca capital of Cuzco ruined and its buildings used as foundation stones for a new city. The price was the disappearance of a complex, cultivated society with an advanced architectural heritage and a wealth of artistry in textiles and decorative crafts. The Incas still inspire and their legacy lives on, to a degree, in the designs and motifs of other Latin American artisans. Yet the loss of the Incas was a sign of how completely and easily the reality of an ancient, indigenous culture could be purposefully destroyed, leaving a mythology that is simply a shadow of long-past glory.

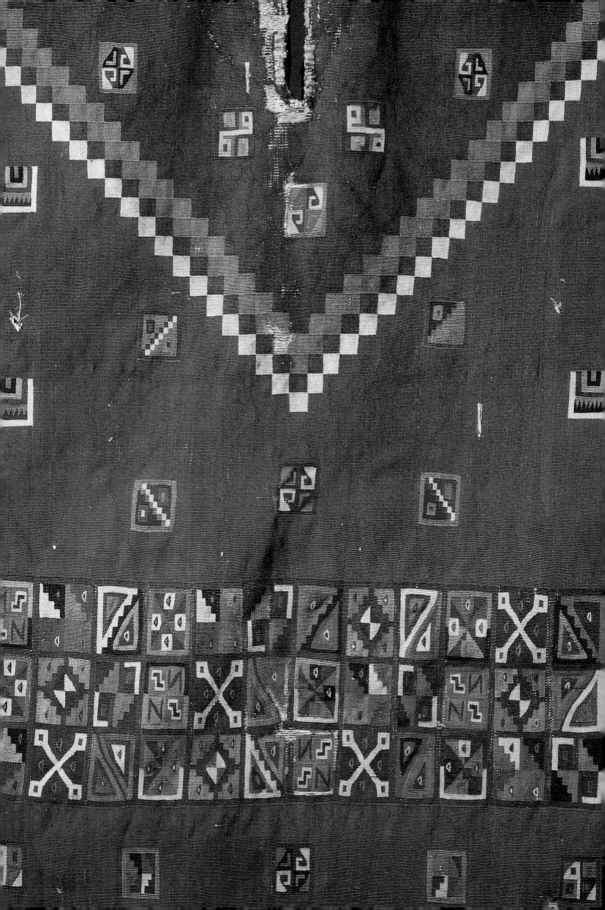

The Incas were experts in scale. They created an immense empire, centred upon Peru but stretching far to the south and east, and they built in a monumental way, sometimes in the most inaccessible of locations.

Forerunners of the Incas, such as the Nazcas, also designed on the grandest of canvases, carving images of hummingbirds and human forms into the earth, drawings hundreds of feet long and so vast they could be seen by the gods above. But there was also symmetry along with scale, the symmetry of the tiered ziggurat architecture and ordered construction. On the modest plan of the home, scale and symmetry are all-important, especially the drama that comes from contrasts of scale – the instant fascination and visual appeal of oversizing a sofa, a table, a fireplace. Or adding a striking element to a room with a sculpture, perhaps a wooden carving so much grander than its surroundings that it stands at the heart of the look. Scale should be about contrast, not conformity. And contrast between rich materials and coarse finishes, between opulence and simplicity, is valuable in emphasizing how finer colours, materials and finishes can stand out all the more when partnered with simpler treatments for walls, floors and fabrics.

There is a deceptive quality to the artistry of Inca design. To us Inca architecture, such as still survives, can look raw and naïve, certainly not fine in the way that, say, Chartres Cathedral is fine.

But then you realize that among the ruins of the Inca capital of Cuzco there are the remnants of great buildings made of dressed stone so carefully cut and laid that a sheet of paper can barely be slipped between the blocks.

At Machu Picchu, Inca architects planned the mountain city so carefully that windows and doorways frame the views of far-away mountain tops, turning the landscape into a series of perfectly composed pictures.

There is a real complexity and subtlety to Inca design that is not always immediately obvious, and the more you look, the more you see.

This architectural and decorative sophistication was the expression of a towering empire. It stretched from Ecuador in the north down through Peru – which we think of as the heartland of Inca civilization – and across Bolivia and down towards Santiago, Chile, to the south. It was an empire that expanded rapidly from the eleventh century onwards, reaching its peak in the fifteenth century, with the capital of Cuzco encircled by a complicated network of satellite cities, all linked by a network of roads and trails over 15,000 miles long, often cut across the mountain passes of the Andes. Relays of runners could carry information across the empire in days, from the coast to the mountains, from the rainforests to the plains.

The Incas developed a monumental approach to architecture, their cities intricately planned and sensibly ordered around palaces and temples, with a sympathetic arrangement of plazas, storehouses, halls and houses. Apart from a ziggurat style for grander buildings, Inca architects worked with trapezoidal windows and grand doorways and added sequences of niches and alcoves for icons. The cities developed as centres for religion and government, but there were also many other towns and communities where the Incas worked not just in dressed stone but also uncut stone set in mortar and simple adobe. At Pisac there are the ruins of an Inca settlement sloping down to the Urubamba River with a steep series of farmland terraces and walls to hold back the river banks: the Incas were highly skilled in creating complicated networks of irrigation channels and aqueducts.

The empire itself was the culmination of forty centuries of development among the Mesoamérican peoples – the ancestors of the Incas, including the Nazcas, the Chavin and also, to the north, the Aztecs and the Maya. The legacy of many of these civilizations is as profound as that of the Incas. Look at the Mayan jungle city of Tikal in Guatemala, for instance, with its great pyramid temples dating back to the seventh century, or the Great Pyramid of Chichén Itzá on Mexico's Yucatán Peninsula alongside the beautiful Temple of Warriors, surrounded by its rows of stone columns standing like a guardian army. Also Uxmal on the Yucatán, where the palaces are covered with vast mosaics of ornate stone friezes, and the pyramids at the Aztec city of Teotihuacan, Mexico, which are often compared to their Egyptian cousins.

With the Incas we are often left to put together our own picture of the grandeur of the empire's achievements because so much of its architecture and wealth was destroyed by the Spanish as they overwhelmed the Incas in the 1530s. The Spanish conquerors of the sixteenth century were obsessive about the riches of the Incas and the hunt for El Dorado, a mythical city of gold they were convinced lay hidden in the depths of the Americas. Yet the Incas themselves were very level-headed about such metals and gems. To them, gold was simply another material to be used as their artistry dictated, especially in the decoration of temples and places of worship. The city of Cuzco was torn apart by the Spanish and its buildings used as the foundations for a new, European-style city, while other Peruvian cities were also looted for gold and precious prizes. Some were simply abandoned as the empire disintegrated. At sites such as Ollantaytambo, large-scale construction was still going on as the Spanish approached and great cut building blocks lie abandoned in fields en route to the city.

The collapse of the Incas was sudden and absolute. The Inca kings were thought to be earthly descendants of their sun god and were revered, their power partly expressed in the form of lavish palaces in Cuzco along with a string of royal estates. Yet the last Inca emperor, Atawalpa, was captured by the Spanish in 1532 and ransomed to his people for a great collection of gold and silver. A year after the king's ransom was delivered, Atawalpa was executed as his kingdom crumbled.

But we still have a romantic, subjective idea of the Incas settled in a startling geography, and that image has an immense charm to it. We also have the solid ruins of many cities, such as the religious centre and royal estate of Machu Picchu discovered in the Urubamba Valley, high up in the Andes, by Hiram Bingham in 1911.

The ruins of many Inca settlements were dug over and further damaged by centuries of treasure hunters searching for clues to the location of El Dorado. However, cities such as Machu Picchu – together with the semi-preserved sacrificial victims of the Incas – do give us a rich vein of truth about the culture and its artistic achievements.

Apart from their skill in crafting stone, and their experience in architectural symmetry and scale, we know some of the motifs and colours that fascinated the Incas. Remnants of friezes and murals depict condors, pumas and llamas, while vivid Inca pottery uses similar stylized animals and birds along with simple, symmetrical patterns. Intricate masks and crowns along with statuary suggest the Incas were highly skilled at working with metals – not just gold but also silver, copper and bronze. And preserved feather headdresses found at sacrificial sites suggest a love of earthy, natural colours such as reds and yellows.

But it is the artistry of Inca textiles that especially fascinates us. The Incas thought cloth superior to gold and silver and more valuable. There was no written language in Inca society and the closest they got to recorded communication – apart from the symbolism used in their designs – was a system related to textiles. Quipu was an unorthodox method of accounting consisting of a central cord of cotton or wool with many coloured and knotted cords tied onto it, forming a complex text for record keeping.

Inca textiles and embroidery – in vibrant shades of red, orange and yellow –

feature geometric patterns and stylized animal motifs as well as more abstract symbols such as stars, and they are sometimes further embellished with fringes and tassels. The Incas used the backstrap looms still in common use among some Peruvian Indians, and worked with many kinds of yarn including cotton and alpaca. The llama was valued across the Andes for its wool and meat, and also as a good pack animal.

In the stylized motifs of the Incas there's a heritage of design that one can easily see in the textiles and geoglyphs – the vast shapes of animals, spiders, birds and men carved into the ground over many hundreds of feet – of their Nazca ancestors, who flourished around 2,000 years ago.

We also see some of that same skill and imagery in the modern-day descendants of the Incas – the Peruvian and Latin American Indians of the Andes broadly labelled as the Quechua – and their more commercial designs based on the same familiar references: hummingbirds and llamas, stars and arrows in bold shades of red, blue and russet, as well as black.

There is a growing Latin American influence – not solely in terms of design – as the region gradually gains in importance and prominence. South American writing and music are more influential than ever, while the West now looks to the rainforest and its peoples for help in finding traditional plant-based treatments for a range of illnesses and complaints.

The Inca influence – compared to the design cultures of India, Africa and other parts of the world – is less pronounced, but the importance of Latin American style in a far broader sense is clearly going to become increasingly significant. And the hope is that this will continue to include the legacy of cultures such as the Incas and Nazcas, together with that of the interlinked craftsmanship of contemporary Indian cultures. Yet, as we are all too aware, indigenous tribal and Indian societies across Latin America are under threat like their counterparts in many other parts of the globe. These are today's disappearing tribes.

Part of the increasing appeal of Inca imagery in textile design is that, like some of the culture's architecture, there is a pleasing simplicity that has an air of modernity about it, despite being steeped in history. In its symmetrical cohesion and strong colours, Inca motifs have an almost digitalized structure, yet they feel organic at the same time. With this mixture of ethnicity and modernity there is a great flexibility to the design, rather like lacquerware or porcelain which can also feel very contemporary and traditional at one and the same time. The colours and imagery of Inca-style fabrics blend well into the more formalized atmosphere that suits much Japanese and Chinese design, but also sit well with the less polished, more rustic look of Thai or Indian furniture. And the pattern is so striking that a cushion, a throw or perhaps a bed-covering can be enough to gain an impact.

More generally, we take other ideas from Inca and Latin America culture. Native headdresses have a striking beauty; their colour and simplicity have great decorative appeal and can work effectively when framed. They create a story, an association, a treat for the eye. And we tend to create our own recesses for use not as sacred spaces, but for displaying artefacts and treasures decoratively, granting them some of the same attention that religious icons and symbols might have received in the past. From Mexico and other countries,

serapes – the blanket-like shawls widely worn by Latin American men – are now increasingly bought for use as thin rugs, bed covers or throws in strong and simple patterns, while the many strong colours used in Mexican and Central American interiors are also becoming very influential. Alpaca wool is being used commercially more than ever before, for both fashion and home.

The expectation has to be that the authority and personality of Latin American design has yet to make its real impact upon the fields of both fashion and the home internationally, but it's inevitable that one day it will.

A Quechua woman dressed in poncho and hat at the window of her adobe house in the Apurimac region of Peru.

A drummer in a dramatic red and blue feathered headdress plays the drums at a dance.

Intense pinks and purples dominate the geometric designs of textiles from the Highlands of Guatemala, Central America.

These intricately crafted wall paintings found at Teotihuacan in Mexico show a mythical figure with a headdress, and date from between the third and sixth centuries AD.

The cut stone walls of the Inca ruins at Pisaq, near Cuzco, Peru, by the Urubama River.

The simple structure of a church exterior with a bell tower is painted in vibrant red.

The stone walls of the Santa Catalina Monastery, Arequipa, Peru, painted red.

A llama herd at Villacayma in the Oruru region of Bolivia. Llamas are used throughout the Andes not just for their alpaca wool but as pack animals and a source of food.

The carved stonework of Aztec antiquities in Mexico. The carving veers from geometric simplicity to the intricate craftsmanship of the curled stone snake, with its forked tongue.

Stylised llamas and other animals mix with bold zigzag patterns in this Tarabuco Indian weaving from Sucre in Bolivia.

The reds, browns, blues and purples of ponchos enliven a marketplace in the Chimborazo province of Ecuador.

Intricate patterns are used to decorate this woven material.

The terraced ruins of Machu Picchu, one of the most famous of the lost Inca cities discovered by Hiram Bingham in 1911.

A Huilloc Indian in the Cuzco region of Peru, dressed in a poncho of rich reds and oranges, takes away a plate of baked potatoes at lunchtime.

Villagers of Saqusilli in the Cotopaxi province of Ecuador travel to the market by truck.

Rich reds dominate the ponchos and hats of these Huilloc villagers watching a festival near Cuzco, Peru, the old Inca capital.

Raj

India is the country of colour.

Jaipur in Rajasthan is considered India's Pink City; the Blue City is Jodhpur. In Goa houses are often painted indigo or white. Even the mud and thatch huts of the farmers of Orissa are beautifully decorated with patterns made with a white paste paint. And everywhere there is that affluence of colour that comes through in the spices, the dress and the coloured, powdered faces of the country's holy men. In a country of 900 million people there is a startling diversity – stark contrasts between opulence and destitution – yet everywhere across India you see this constant love of ornamentation, a love of colour. From the days of the Raj and before, Westerners have been taken aback by this brash, confident use of paint and pigment. And over the course of the years the Indian approach to colour has helped to revolutionize Western attitudes. But India is not just about the range of its painter's palette – the country has an ancient, monumental architecture too, and a wealth of sophisticated style to its countless palaces, town houses and houseboats.

Across India there are few homes which have separate rooms for dining and entertaining.

It is more traditional to have one large living room that serves both purposes, an informal space for relaxing and eating with low-level seating such as a baithak – a padded mattress positioned against a wall, with cushions to support the back. At the same time there are very few internal doors to the Indian home, emphasizing its informality while also allowing air to circulate around the house. The influence of this style can be seen in contemporary Western interiors, where there is a tendency towards the informality of the combined living and dining room, as well as a move towards a more informal floor plan. As in Japan and other parts of Indo-China and the East, in India elevating oneself above others in the home is, or was, seen as impolite, while the natural level was always the ground. In the cities, especially, where space is at a premium, a separate dining room is often a luxury and many prefer one large, well-designed space similar to the Indian model.

And privacy in the home is now less of an issue – barrier doorways to living rooms, bedrooms and even bathrooms are slowly disappearing as we feel less and less of a need to lock ourselves away from our partners and families.

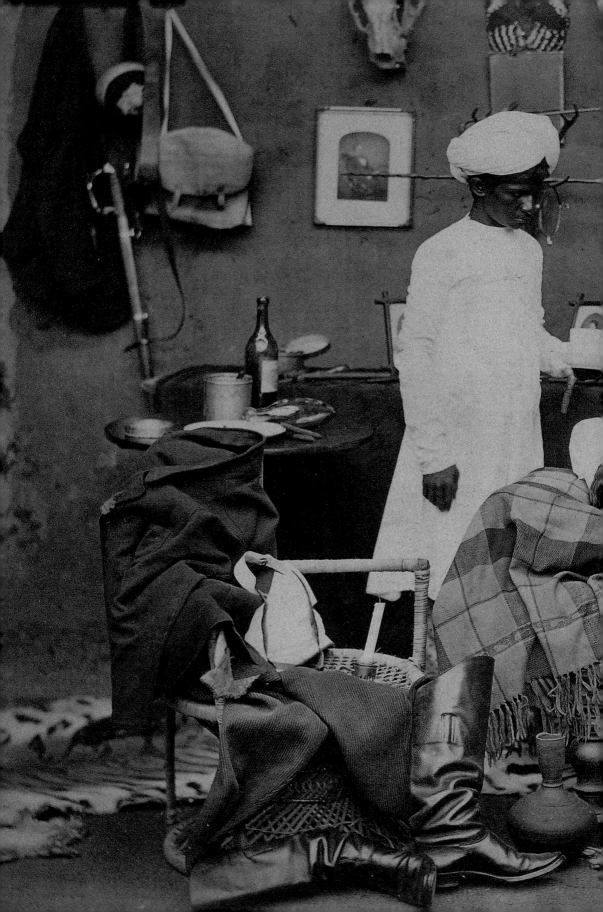

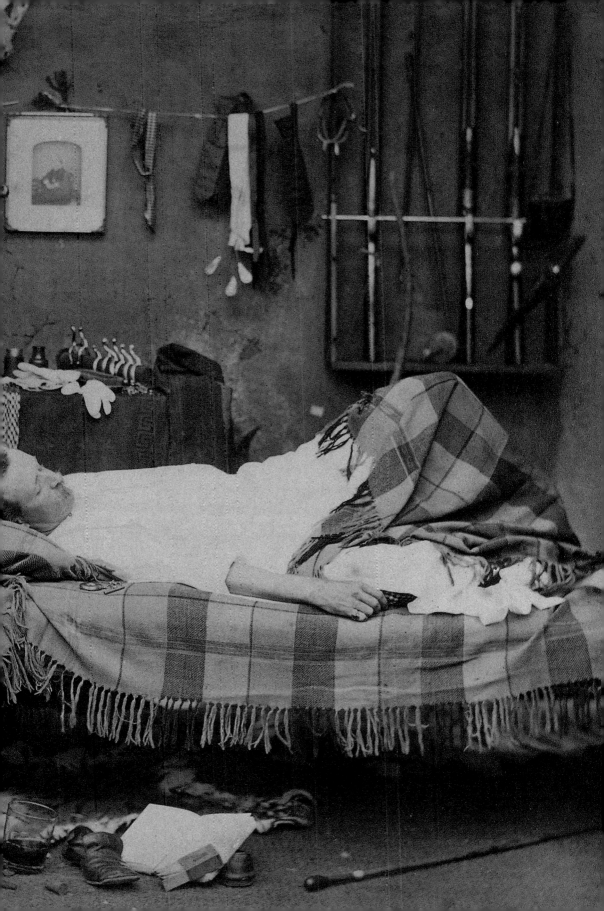

India assaults the senses. The sounds and smells of the whirling machine of Indian society, its sights and colours, its people – they all leave an indelible impression on the mind of any traveller. And the country has become one of the great modern travel destinations, not just an obligatory tour for the backpackers of the world or a sojourn stop-over for pleasure seekers savouring the beaches around Goa or Cochin.

For anyone seeking experiences and memories, India is tempting as there is such a deep mine of culture, design and architecture, stretching through time.

Every image, sight and photograph is etched with colour. Colours are everywhere, decoration is everywhere: a bright and exuberant film poster; the deep colours of spices laid out on trays in every marketplace; the painted faces of holy men and Hindu icons; the scarlets and indigos of shimmering saris; the ornately decorated buses of Kerala and the exotic murals painted across Karnataka bullock carts. Colour is universal and the home is no exception.

Jaipur is known as the Pink City of Rajasthan, with many of its houses washed with pale shades of red. It is also renowned for the quality of its ceramics. The province's capital, Jaipur, was one of India's first great modern cities, planned in the eighteenth century by the Moghul Maharaja, Jai Singh II, who also created the opulent Chadra Maha, or Moon Palace. The Palace itself is a hymn to colour and ornamental excess: the cool blue and white frescoes and polished shining stucco floor of the Hall of Images; the mirror-encrusted walls and ceilings of the Hall of Beauty, with their floral patterns made from gold leaf and coloured tinsel topped by glass for a reflective riot of rainbow tones. Everywhere there are gold and jewel colours, reds, greens and pinks in ceramic tiles, mica glass and painted, patterned walls.

The fortress city of Jodhpur, Rajasthan, is the Blue City, sitting on the edge of the vast Thar Desert and with a long history as a great trading centre. Blue paint washes for the town houses – the *haveli* – of the superior Brahmin caste once served to mark them apart, a colour of rank and wealth. Today the cool, fresh blues have a wider, more democratic appeal among Jodhpuris, but still help to give the city some of its unique character. And the blues seep into the interiors, too; the mix of indigo colours and whitewash cooling and refreshing in the heat.

In Goa in the south, it's also common to find homes painted in shades of indigo and blue, or in simple whites.

At Jaisalmer, on the edge of the Thar Desert, farmers' mud homes have an organic simplicity, rising from the earth, with whitewash used sparingly to create geometric motifs and frames for windows and doorways.

Similarly in Orissa, mud and thatch huts are decorated outside and in with more complex designs featuring stylized vines, fields and harvested rice grain piled high into pyramids. These are the simplest of homes, yet they are proudly and artistically adorned.

Elsewhere in India there is a tradition of ornate, painted woodwork for home interiors. Across houses in the Ladakh Mountains to the north you see architraves, beams and wooden panels painted with patterns and frescoes using bold, primary colours that dominate with their intensity, depicting icons, religious stories and historical scenes. Fables and spiritual tales also feature on the front doors of some *havelis* in Rajasthan, the bright paints standing out against the dark backdrop of the wood.

The use of colour in India has a multitude of complicated religious connotations, many related to Hinduism.

Blue is associated with Krishna, Vishnu, the sustainer, and also the face of Shiva, the destroyer. Surya, the sun deity, is often represented by the colours of the rainbow; Kali, the destroyer, by black. Hanuman, the monkey god, is linked to green, while Agni, the fire god, is associated with red, as are the robes of Vishnu's consort, Lakshmi.

Colour has a language all of its own, used as an intrinsic part of pilgrimages, religious festivals and ceremonies as well as being tied to the caste system which permeates Hindu culture.

The red tika dots on the foreheads of Hindu women are made of vermilion paste, while brides traditionally cover their faces in turmeric and decorate their palms with henna as they prepare for marriage. During the spring festival of

Holi revellers coat one another in the streets with an intense cerise dye. Holy men, or sadhus, and dancers cover their faces in bold masks of paint – blues, yellows, reds. And garlands of intense, bright marigolds decorate doorways and are used as wedding decorations.

In dress, too, a broad intensity of colour can be seen in Indian saris and turbans, blazing cottons and embroidered shawls. Everyday clothing involves a rainbow of bright colours, and even the simple cotton wraps of the sadhus are in intense shades of yellow, red and blue. Tribal costumes from Kerala to Rajasthan revel in colour and pattern. The nomadic Rabari people of Gujarat and Rajasthan use colour to enrich their temporary mud and clay huts while their traditional ornate dress is in the richest indigos, opulent purples and scarlets.

For the English Victorians of the Raj the Indian attitude to colour was a shock. In Georgian and early Victorian England there was a restrained, conservative approach to colour and a tradition of adopting relatively muted tones. Even when chinoiserie patterns and the richer, deeper colours of Oriental china and lacquer began to become popular from the seventeenth and eighteenth centuries onwards, the use of paint pigments remained very limited. And the same was true of many other countries in the West where traditional methods for making distemper led to very chalky, flat shades across the paint palette. In India the use of richer, spicier colours in a whole variety of contexts – from food to ritual to decoration – slowly began to influence the Victorians and still has an effect on us today.

In contemporary interior design in the West, the power of colour has yet to be fully appreciated and still has a tendency towards an inconspicuous, reserved approach.

One of the down sides of the growth of minimalism in architecture and design was that it needlessly tended to deny the power and drama of colour, although we are now starting to see a reaction to that mood and a far more experimental spirit creeping in, partly inspired by the continuing example of ethnic design cultures such as that to be found across India. Partly through our mistakes, we are gradually learning never to underestimate the impact of colour upon a room, not just in paints but in fabrics, furniture and textural materials such as exposed brick and varnished woods.

Colour has to be the single most powerful expression of style, creating an instant atmosphere and ambience as well as the creative framework for a room.

Darker, richer colours such as red and indigo create warmth and intimacy. Lighter, brighter colours such as yellow and lilac may well help to open up a space, while neutrals create a foundation for experimenting with texture and colour through upholstered furniture, curtains and finishes. Colour can very often be the key to tying the look of a room together, yet it can also help to ruin it by overwhelming the space or draining it of life.

It is the most important and difficult choice to make in decorating any room. And given that so much else depends on it, one hopes to get it right. Reassurance comes from the fact that there is no law against experimenting with all kinds of colours and contrasts before deciding. Even if it turns out to be wrong, there's no easier way to change the look of a room than by simply repainting a wall.

In India there is a widespread confidence in the use of colour in design and within the home, a confidence that seems to come from experience. Experience in understanding what kind of colours suit particular spaces – light for light areas, dark for dark – mixed with a relative lack of restraint and a common tendency towards drama. It's a cumulative experience which expresses itself in India's arts and crafts, its textiles, its craftsmanship in stone, wood, ceramics and glass work, as well as in its architecture and interiors. There is, after all, a long and accomplished history to Indian design and architecture stretching back over a thousand years.

As in many other cultures, the early impetus in India towards designing and building on an accomplished and grandiose scale was tied up with religion, as well as power and patronage. From the fifth century right through to the eighteenth – when the British began to tighten their grip on the country – countless temples were built across India, many on a huge scale. The Hindu temples were primarily homes for the gods more than places of worship, so were designed in the hope that they would suit and please the gods on earth. The earliest temples were cut right into the rock itself. At Mamallapuram, by the coast in Tamil Nadu, seventh-century stonemasons carved the temples from standing blocks of pink granite, creating extraordinary temple structures and images of the gods in the monoliths, together with carved lions and elephants. Only the Shore Temple, built a hundred or so years later, with its two carved towers, was built of cut stone.

The temple at Elephanta, not far from Bombay, was also cut from the rock like an immense sculpture – columns, porticoes, lions and all. Kailasa Temple at Ellora, Maharashtra, was created in the eighth century and was an astonishing accomplishment, carved right down into the mountain rock so you look down at this vast structure excavated deep into the stone, surrounded by vaulted galleries.

The Surya (Sun God) Temple at Konarak on the Bay of Bengal, Orissa, was built much later, around the thirteenth century. It was so colossal and heavy – and as much as 40 metres (130 feet) high – that much of it collapsed in the nineteenth century. The surviving section, built in the form of a vast sun chariot, is complete with great carved stone wheels and decorated with stone elephants – one of India's most sacred animals, with a mythology all of its own – horses and nymphs, along with sequences of erotic carvings. Achievements like the Surya Temple rivalled, perhaps exceeded, anything being built in Europe at the time.

Also dating from the thirteenth century, the city of Varanasi, in Uttar Pradesh, is home to the Golden Temple – or Vishwanath.

The Golden Temple is covered with 800 kilograms (almost 1,800 pounds) of gold plating and is the greatest wonder of this holiest of Hindu cities. Sited on the banks of the Ganges, Varanasi has miles of stone stairways leading down to the river for bathing in a ritual of purification. Across the city there are over a thousand golden shrines, and to die in Varanasi is regarded a great spiritual blessing.

In the seventeenth century, just as the British East India Company (with its tight grip on trade between England, India and the Far East) began to make its presence felt, the Minakshi Sundareshvara Temple was constructed at Madurai, Tamil Nadu. A great Dravidian (India's aboriginal peoples) temple dedicated to Shiva and his consort, Parvati, the temple is an extended maze of courtyards and galleries reached through giant gopurams, or carved gateways, that sit like multicoloured mountains, covered in brightly painted images of divinities, animals and praying figures. The detail and intricacy are as disarming as the colours, which are refreshed every year, and the gateways can be seen from almost anywhere in the city.

Also by the seventeenth century, the Moslem Moghul emperor, Babur, followed by his son, Akbar, had begun to bring India together as one cohesive empire, as well as to encourage architecture, painting and the arts and crafts to new heights of expression. The Indian empire under Akbar – 'the great Moghul' – was one of the greatest in the world, and among the most sophisticated and well-governed, out-rivalling that of his contemporary, Queen Elizabeth I. Akbar's son, Jahangir, was another supporter of the arts, and the next in line, Shah Jahan, built the Taj Mahal (1632–43) as a mausoleum for his favourite wife, its marble walls inlaid with jewels and perhaps the greatest example of Islamic art in the whole of India. And it was Shah Jahan who also built – in the 1640s and 1650s – the Jama Masjid mosque in Delhi, the largest in the country, made with repeating strips of sandstone and marble and twin minarets standing 40 metres (130 feet) high.

The decline and disintegration of the Moghul empire and its system of government, alongside European trade and political rivalries, led India towards a different kind of rule that finally culminated in the British Raj. The Raj was established in the late eighteenth and early nineteenth centuries. By the 1830s India's official language was English, as was the rest of the state structure, and the Moghul rulers were an anachronism.

While the rule of the British did not put a stop to the rich tradition of artistry and design promoted and encouraged by Moslem emperors and Hindu maharajas alike, it did make an indelible impression upon India in countless ways. The British Raj did influence the architecture and way of living with its anglicized bungalows, hill stations and examples of high Victorian buildings, such as Sir Edwin Lutyen's parliament buildings in New Delhi and F. W. Steven's Victoria Terminus railway station in Bombay.

The English way of dining and relaxing also influenced Indian furniture makers, who began crafting Westernized pieces as well as traditional Indian designs.

But the pattern of trade and influence was a two-way process, as it always had been. The whole foundation of the British Raj lay with the trading links pioneered by the British East India Company, initially interested in Indian cotton and spices. This growing Indian influence upon Britain – as well as other parts of Europe – was certainly not restricted to lessons in exotic colour. Perhaps the greatest impact upon British design was to do with textiles, with many of the traditional motifs, colours and patterns of Indian fabrics taken up and reproduced by British manufacturers.

Chintz, the classic fabric of the picture-book English country cottage, is derived from an Indian block-printed cotton.

The name itself is taken from the Sanskrit word *chitra*, meaning speckled. Paisley, similarly, was a design common to Kashmiri textiles using the stylized mango motif within a floral design, renamed after the Scottish mill town which adopted the pattern as its own in the seventeenth century. The commercial cultivation of cotton itself is thought to have first begun in India; calico is named after Calicut on the coast of Kerala. And the block-printed and hand-painted cottons imported from India were also among the first fabrics to have the luxury and practicality of holding permanent colour while also being washable.

Indian textiles and embroidery continue to be popular, although the tendency today is certainly away from anglicized chintz towards what we tend to think of as more ethnic designs: batiks and ikats, such as patola from Orissa and Andhra Pradesh; southern Indian silk brocades; the zardozhi sequin-covered embroidery common to Uttar Pradesh; Kashmiri crewelwork; the crocheted textiles of Gujarat and the mirror-work fabrics of Gujarat and Rajasthan. Embroidery is one of India's great decorative arts, incorporating sequins, silver and gold thread with motifs such as elephants, birds, deer and lotus flowers – the latter being a sacred bloom in Hinduism, its stem reaching down to the spiritual depths of the earth. Silk saris in bright colours from Tamil Nadu, Orissa and other parts of India are used not just as clothing but as curtain fabric, tablecloths and throws.

The colours, patterns and types of Indian textiles, the choice of cottons, linens, velvets and jacquards, are so rich and varied that they have made their way across the world for centuries and have been endlessly copied and reworked. Finer silks and embroideries are used as wall hangings and bed covers, other stronger, hard-wearing weaves for upholstery.

Many contemporary designs are still inspired by the motifs of Indian fabrics especially those using floral patterns, sun symbols and Mughal imagery.

Indian carpets and rugs are still much in demand – cotton dhurries in geometric designs, coir mats from Kerala and finer, far more elaborate woven carpets of the kind first introduced to India by the Mughal emperors, using Persian patterns and symbols including varieties of vines, flowers and fruits.

Indian furniture, especially its worked wooden designs, has also become increasingly popular and is widely exported.

Traditional Indian furniture means low tables to complement the ornate mattresses – or *baithaks* – that surround the edges of a room, with cushions against the wall to support the back.

In the days of the Raj, Indian furniture makers adopted a much wider repertoire, creating Westernized designs which then became commonplace for Indian homes. This resulted in a wealth of well-made, Victorian-style Indian furniture as well as more modern designs from the twentieth century: dining chairs and tables, cabinets and armchairs in Anglo-Indian fusions along with wickerwork and cane sofas – the classic furnishings of the verandah. The common use of pearl and ivory veneers and inlays in Indian design meant that the craftsmanship could be very fine, and finishes still range from a very rustic, unpolished look to exquisite and elaborate detailing.

Other Indian styles of furniture have been adopted by the West, such as the divan, with the word taken from the Persian *diwan*. Similarly, large swing chairs, supported by chains fixed to the ceiling and found in some grander Indian houses and palaces, have permeated through to many Western and American verandahs and porches, although they are much more dramatic and elegant when situated indoors. Indian swing chairs are often elaborately carved and crafted, offering an enticing centre point to a room.

More generally, the diversity of Indian architecture, with its rich mixture of traditions, has had a real effect upon Western interiors, partly through the medium of the Raj.

Some strands of Anglo-Indian domestic architecture tried to combine Indian approaches to design with suburban familiarity, as British architects and designers looked for ways to cope with the Indian climate. The blurring between outside and in, common to many Indian houses, translated into a wide adoption of verandahs and decks, terraces and balconies, allowing air to circulate. It was a way of living which then gradually filtered back home and was applied to some English homes. The use of bare wooden floors in teak, rose or sandalwood – appreciated for its cooling qualities – was also important, with less of an emphasis on carpets and rugs.

The whole system of purdah – the segregation of women tied to Hindu and Muslim tradition – meant the development of other architectural models, such as a sophisticated system of internal and screened windows. Jalis are pierced, latticework panels incorporated into window arches allowing air to circulate and, to some extent, a view outwards, but with hardly a glimpse to be had in through the lattice from outside. Made with intricately carved stone or woodwork, jalis are a common architectural feature, their patterns and motifs copied into many more contemporary designs. Many jali windows were inside the home or palace and the use of internal windows, which allows light to pass through interior spaces, is becoming increasingly common in Western architecture as people try to maximize all available light and space.

Other architectural features, such as shutters, windows, carved screens and doors, have been incorporated into the design of Western contemporary interiors just as they are, using the pieces as decorative focal points. These include intricately carved doors, ancient and worn, from places such as Chettinad, near Madurai in Tamil Nadu, famous for the careful craftsmanship of its heavy, wooden panelled doors; the jharokhas – beautifully carved, wooden windows found in Rajasthan and Gujarat; even panelling, such as the kind found on the houseboats of Kashmiri, renowned for its skilled carpenters. The grain of the wood and the texture that comes with age gives such pieces a character and history that can work well in the melange of fusion style, while the sheer drama of scale has an importance in itself.

Other more ornamental crafts can also be an inspiration. The use of stained glass and mica – which one associates with Islamic influences also to be seen in the design style of the Maghreb – reaches astonishing levels of brilliance in the palaces of many Indian princes and maharajas. The painting of images and portraits, icons and symbols, onto glass – common across India – gives the images a glowing translucence similar to early, colour-tinted daguerreotypes. The use of mirrorwork is not limited to textiles and the walls of palaces, but is also used in the decoration of more accessible homes. The Banni tribe of Gujarat, for instance, uses pieces of mirror set into the clay and lime walls of its simple roundhouses.

Everywhere there is this love of ornamentation and decorative excess, and we take note of the elements and ideas we love and leave others behind. Often this excess is tempered by a patina of age, which frequently adds extra layers of character and interest.

We don't want the new, mass-produced charpoy – the lightweight Indian bed, often adapted as a low sofa – but the old, worn version, scuffed and marked but full of associations.

We sometimes see in fading plaster and distressed paintwork an added charm, leading to a whole discipline in contemporary design where we look to distress, roughen and score walls and floors, moving away from the perfect finish to find texture and personality in imperfection and thereby achieve a more rustic look. It's about faded grandeur and character. India excels in both.

The endless diversity of Indian style makes it such a source of ideas and inspiration, colours, textiles, furniture and objects for merging into the look of our own homes. The contrast between sophistication and rusticity, opulence and simplicity, fine finishes and faded tones, results in a general sense of flexibility. Fine Islamic influences and motifs mixing with the exuberance and artistry of Hindu style and the colourful ethnic simplicity of the Indian tribal cultures mean that you can find connections between elements of Indian design and those of other cultures with comparative ease.

The finesse of India's Islamic style – its textiles, glasswork, carpets, motifs – sits naturally with North African and Persian influences, but also with the more formal, crafted qualities of Chinese and even Japanese design. The less refined elements of tribal India, on the other hand, with its more rustic take on furniture and woodwork – from charpoys to door frames – merge well with the styles of Indo-China, Indonesia and sub-Saharan Africa.

The long-established Anglo-Indian fusions that came through trade and the Raj – in furniture especially, but also textiles – can also be seen in amalgamations of English, European and Western interior design with Indian influences. Some of the romanticized imagery of the Raj, too – from sepia photographs of howdah-topped elephants to papier-mâché tigers, punkah fans and old hurricane lanterns – still has charm and such touches are sometimes adopted. The legacy of the Raj is still with us, as it is with India. Just think of commonly used words, such as jodhpurs, khaki, polo and pyjamas – all originated in India and were filtered through the medium of the Raj.

Even though one feels there's a sense of timelessness to life in India, that India is a country largely held hostage by its past – culturally, politically, economically – there is always a valuable and unique creative vibrancy to be found there.

In terms of arts and crafts, design and architecture, India has long been a great influence upon Europe, as well as other parts of the world, such as Indo-China.

There is such a respect for craftsmanship and artistry, a love of ornament and colour, that stretches right through the society from top to bottom. Like South America, one feels that India's influence is still making itself felt as Indian design continues to grow and reinvent itself.

The soft red stone tiers of the Palace of the Winds in Jaipur, Rajasthan, also known as India's Pink City.

A carved stone elephant along with a monkey and panther form part of a latticed window in Gwalior, Madhya Pradesh.

Bright red chilli peppers spill from sacking bags.

Marigolds for sale at a flower market in Varanasi, the Hindu holy city in Uttar Pradesh, on the banks of the Ganges.

The interior of the Golden Temple at Amritsar, in the Punjab, in 1857. It is a focus for the Sikh religion and most Sikhs try to bathe in its waters at least once in their lives.

Two girls entertain themselves with a picnic under a tree.

An ornate stonework panel decorates a Hindu temple.

A male servant looks after the master – probably an army officer – in Burma in 1885.

A painted scene showing a public gathering and celebration.

Crowds of men and women in brightly coloured turbans and saris at festival time in the streets of Pushkar, Rajasthan.

Servants at work outside in the market square, one of a series of photographs taken by Lieut. Col. W.W. Hooper in Mandalay in 1886.

A camel driver from Pushkar, Rajasthan, wearing a bright yellow turban.

Coast

Coast is influenced by the light,

natural look of New England. It is not an ethnic style, like many other elements of fusion interiors, but forms a very specific kind of look and has a definite charisma and power all the same. It was partly shaped by the traditions and ideas brought to the region by America's founding fathers in the seventeenth century, yet has become a very distinctive design style in itself. It is the light, airy look of Cape Cod, Martha's Vineyard and Nantucket, with their clapboard houses, sweeping front porches and picket fences. It is a look shaped by the sea, by the elements, with a weather-worn shingle roof and peeling, whitewashed wooden boards at the gable ends. Coast is rooted in the American Dream, especially the golden era of the 1950s when there was a confidence to American values and the Kennedys laid the foundations for Camelot from the warmth of their reassuring Cape Cod escape at Hyannis Port. It is the look of an innocent America, shaped by the style and philosophy of the pilgrims and the generations that followed. It is about a wholesome approach to home living, in which escapism combines with Shaker simplicity.

There is a startling quality and clarity of light across New England.

It is something that attracts home owners, photographers and painters alike. Painter Edward Hopper captured a classic, crisp, cinematic vision of the coast through images of Maine and Cape Cod in the 1920s, 1930s and 1950s. Colour and texture acquire a special clarity along the coast north of New York, up to Maine and the border with Canada. Throughout the houses you see a use of light colours – whites or light greys for exteriors and yellows, pale greens and any shades of white and cream for interiors. No dark, sombre colours will suit. The principle here is the same as anywhere: light colours suit light spaces, dark colours suit darker, more intimate rooms. It is a myth that light colours can simply transform a dark interior. The effect is always minimal and the brightness of the colours simply recedes with the low levels of light, because shades can look so very different in varying exposures. It is always best to appreciate and to fit in with the mood and atmosphere of the room itself, and only through tending to the sources of light is it possible to alter the basics of a room's tone.

Nowhere in America will you find more patrician-like houses, parks and gardens more opulent, than in New Bedford. Whence came they? How planted upon this country? Go and gaze upon the iron emblematical harpoons round yonder lofty mansions, and your question will be answered. Yes; all these brave houses and flowery gardens came from the Atlantic, Pacific and Indian oceans.

Herman Melville, from *Moby Dick* (1851).

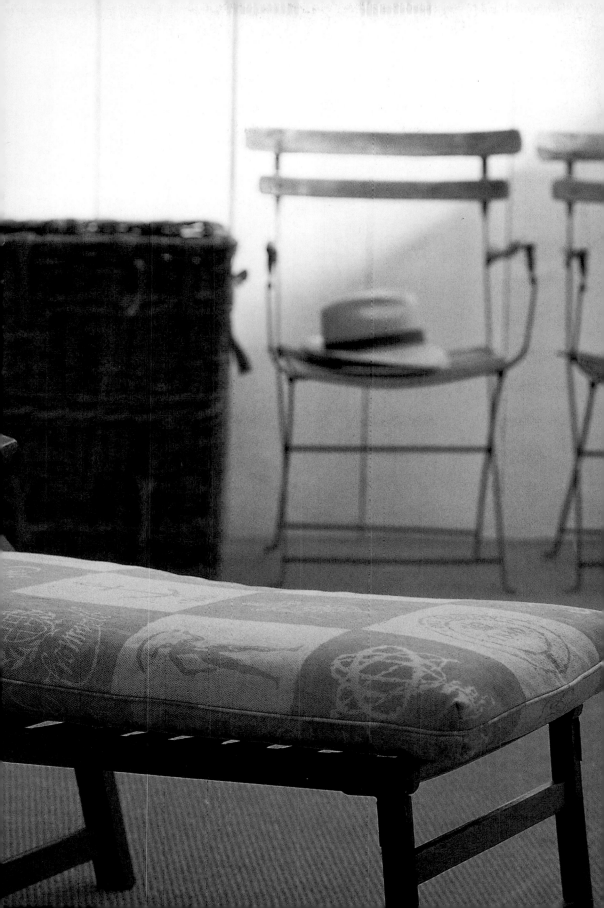

There is a well-known black and white image on the cover of an old copy of *Life* magazine, with John F. Kennedy and his wife on a sailing boat, out on the water, looking happy, content and carefree. It's an image of the American Dream, of a gleaming, innocent America of the 1950s and early 1960s. An image that somehow sums up the style of the East Coast, of New England, as much as Edward Hopper's paintings of Cape Cod and Maine, with their clapboard houses settled into the landscape and their gleaming lighthouses, white and clean in the sun. They are all images of an America saturated in media myth and fable – the America of picture-perfect houses and picket fences, of the Stars and Stripes, the America of Kennedy's Camelot, of Jimmy Stewart in the small-town saga *It's a Wonderful Life*, and of baseball hero Joe DiMaggio.

Like any good escapist myth, this image of America has its roots in reality. On Cape Cod, Martha's Vineyard and Nantucket there are still the perfect clapboard houses, their wooden fences dipping down towards the beach, partly obscured by sand. America is a different country than it was in the 1950s and before, changed by politics and time. But the idealized image of New England,

of the East Coast, remains powerful and enticing.

This is not an ethnic look, but it does have a strong vein of rusticity. It is a look partly shaped by the sea, the light and the great American outdoors.

It is homely and stylish but not especially sophisticated. It is too simple for that. Nor is it perfect: the paint on the clapboard is weather-worn, leaves need brushing from the porch, the shingles on the roof are a little uneven. Coast is also about the home in the landscape, shaped and moulded by it.

This classic look of New England is, in itself, a kind of fusion between a provincial English way of building brought over by the early settlers and a distinctly American approach to home style.

The early settlers of New England thought they were arriving in a potential utopia, offering the chance to create their own society and their own way of living. The settlers' rush began in the 1630s and by 1700 the population of New England was 100,000, and double that by 1730. Many of these early colonists were devout Puritans, Quakers, Presbyterians and Baptists and, partly through religious belief and partly through circumstance, they adopted a highly communal pattern of life in the early settlements.

They also favoured a simple austerity in building style and even their churches were little more than square wooden blocks, with modest bell towers. Again, this was partly to do with circumstance, and available materials. The wood was there for building while many of the settlers were from agricultural communities and brought with them a practical preference for two-storey, timber-framed homes on a very simple plan, with the two main downstairs living rooms positioned on either side of a central fireplace. The walls were lined with wattle and daub, while pine clapboards were pinned to the outside. A kitchen was built as a lean-to at the back of the house and an enclosed porch was sometimes added to the front.

With a limited number of craftsmen and such a call for construction, carpenters and artisans were in great demand and a tradition developed of healthy respect for the skill and workmanship of New England's craftsmen. Oak was the favoured choice for home building, but there was also walnut and chestnut. Furniture makers desperately tried to meet the need for furnishing these new homes, often working very quickly and to relatively simple designs with little time or opportunity for intricate finishes and detailing.

As a result, in both home building and the look of the interiors of such houses, there was a thread of simplicity and utility which we associate with New England and Shaker style.

There was also a beauty to it, a clarity of form and function and a certain elegant charm. Even as the power of the church declined, trade and wealth increased, and New England society became more liberal and worldly, the basic design of the home remained familiar. By the eighteenth century, as a Classical influence filtered across the Atlantic from Europe, there was some added ornamentation, such as pediments and pilasters around the front door and enriched façades. But the look of basic block building and clapboards remained as New England East Coast style evolved its own distinctive character. Even the grandest houses of the eighteenth century, built in Georgian style, had this innate symmetry to them.

In the look of the classic New England interior the theme of simplicity is carried through.

Even as the layout of homes became more complicated in the eighteenth century – with a four-room floorplan, higher ceilings and larger windows for a greater feeling of space – the simple lines of the rooms, the wood-panelled walls, the plain wooden floors and simple wooden mantelpieces stayed.

The paint colours fit into the palette we now think of as Shaker – whites, blues, yellows – all possessed of a dramatic clarity.

There were also pale greens, greys, light reds – colours which complemented the quality of light along the coastal provinces. There were washes too, using mixtures of soot, egg and buttermilk for a mottled look, and occasional paint effects such as dotted patterning with colour on white or cream, like a Dalmatian's coat, for below the dado rail. Many contemporary paint patterns and washes have been influenced by the recipes used in New England homes.

As time moved on other references and ideas were added to the mix. There was the influence of early Dutch, French and German settlers, as well as the English, but it was the evolution of a true American style that transformed the way we think of New England style. It is now tied up with the idealistic, homely, all-American imagery of the Stars and Stripes on a garden flagpole, the home-made American quilt, rocking chairs on the porch, pieces of driftwood and fishing floats or buoys used as decoration. Again, this is an image filtered through film and fiction, linked to an ideal of a fine, small-town America of the kind found in Frank Capra's film *It's A Wonderful Life*, with its emphasis on the values that hold family and friendship together.

And it remains an incredibly powerful, stylized image. The New England look is no longer confined to America, but has a far wider resonance.

Painted woodwork, clapboard detailing and coloured tongue-and-groove panels, stars and stripes motifs for fabrics, Shaker furniture and particularly Shaker-style kitchens – all are common-place references. The use of decks and verandahs – this intersection between inside and out, similar to some Oriental or Eastern approaches to outside living spaces – has been very influential, often reproduced on the smaller scale of city gardens and terraces.

Modern versions of New England style have mixed the look with exposed brick walls, Victorian claw-foot bathtubs and native Indian artwork.

The stylized feel of the barn conversion in particular fits perfectly with the New England theme, with its basic rusticity and similarity of form to the clapboard home, while providing the opportunity to lay the living rooms out in a very different way. Barn conversions have tended to opt for wide, open-plan living spaces and banks of windows and skylights, making the most of light and space. Yet the language of design can still be one of New England and Shaker simplicity – wood, white walls, exposed beams. The concentration on openness, simplicity and light often results in interiors which can feel contemporary despite being totally rooted in tradition.

Everyday objects such as fishing rods, old children's toys and crafted wooden tools are used decoratively as part of the theme. As with religious icons from the East, African basketry or Japanese ceramic bowls, these are pieces that have gone beyond their original function and are used decoratively because of their powerful associations, the beauty of finish or texture – representatives of another age and stage.

At the same time, New England style creates a simple, neutral foundation for experimenting with texture and splashes of colour in fabrics and upholstery, rather like the Japanese look, yet without its marked formality. Being so much about the use of light, natural colours and paints, even a fresh vase of flowers can stand out as a beacon of colour. A delicate use of occasional floral motifs, splashes of pattern, a stained chequerboard-effect wooden floor, and a coloured glaze for a tile splash-back to protect kitchen and bathroom walls from moisture – all assume a real intensity with such a recessive, light backdrop. Texture shines through in wood, linens and crisp cottons.

This interior style does not suit heavy curtains with eleborate swags and tails, but calls for bare windows with shutters or blinds. Again, the look and grain of the wood – along with that of other natural materials such as bamboo, suedes and leathers – fit in naturally with the emphasis on light and texture. It is a more open way of living which naturally suits the country, although many ideas and themes inspired by New England style have been neatly transplanted to town houses, while the emphasis on maximizing light and texture is something that can be applied to any home.

It is a look that, more than most, relies on colour to tie it together. The choices have to be light, the touch has to be gentle.

In fusion, the rich intensity of Chinese formality, with its lacquer finishes and emphasis on pattern and colour, may simply be too much. Better to opt for the more sympathetic quality of natural materials, such as seagrass and coir, with some ethnic touches in a very restrained use of pattern and a complementary emphasis on texture in crafted wood-work from South East Asia or India. The key ingredients should always tend more towards informality and lightness.

The bright colours of a fluttering American flag stand out boldly against the clean porches and white timbers of these Victorian homes in Cape May, New Jersey.

The painted woodwork and roof timbers of an ocean view home at Cape Neddick, Maine, look crisp against the sea and skyline as a sailboat passes.

The crisp blues and whites of the ocean and surf, along with the neutrality of clear sands, provides inspiration to those who live along the coast.

A climbing rose blooms on the roof and shingles of a home on the island of Nantucket, one of the most picturesque areas of New England.

The rocking chair on the front porch of a simple but elegant clapboard house offers an all-American ideal of country living.

An early issue of *Life* magazine, Issue 29, July 1953, featuring the Kennedy's sailing.

Logos decorate the painted clapboard exterior of a town store.

Fishermen posing with the day's catch, around 1900.

A crudely painted American flag enlivens the rough wooden shell of a shack house antique shop.

Dinghies tied to the dock at a Maine harbour.

A picturesque, timbered village house, complete with classic picket fence.

The cut logs at the corner of an old log cabin suggest simplicity and solid craftsmanship.

Manhattan

When you walk down New York's

Fifth Avenue it's hard not to imagine that you are at the centre of the world, such is the power of Manhattan. Our image of the city, its sights and style, has been shaped by film, by Hollywood, as much as by reality: Cary Grant in *An Affair to Remember*, Fred Astaire in *Top Hat*, Fay Wray in *King Kong*, or the Busby Berkeley excess of *42nd Street*. Its skyline could almost be made of celluloid and has to be the most famous of any metropolis. And for Manhattan the greatest decade has to be the 1930s, the era of the Chrysler Building and the Empire State Building, of Radio City Music Hall, the era of Art Deco sophistication when New York style truly came of age despite the Depression. It was when the Manhattan look really began to come alive – the look of the skyscraper apartment, all sleek finishes and Deco shapes, tailored fabrics and masculine touches. It is the ultimate take on metropolitan living that has since been played out and extended on the broader canvas of the Manhattan loft. Manhattan style is always polished, cosmopolitan and modern.

The key to the constant glamour of the Manhattan look comes from its finishes, its surface glow.

The shine was at its brightest in the Art Deco glory years of the 1930s when the great Parisian-born design movement was given a decidedly New York spin. And the greatest of all Deco finishes has to be chrome: the gleam of highly polished metallics for lights and fixtures, oversized taps and shower heads, steel-framed chairs and mirror frames. There was also the allure of lacquer, with its Oriental flavours, popular for wall panelling, dining tables and liquor cabinets. Manhattan Deco was obsessed with sheen in all its forms, in glass walls and banks of ceramic tiles, varnished parquet and sleek leather. It was touched by fantasy, excess and escapism.

MANHATTAN

The materials of Manhattan Deco still help to shape the look of the city today but in a more mature, considered way. Polished steel for kitchens, leather and lacquer along with the smooth curves of Deco furniture are an intrinsic part of the more contemporary take on New York style.

New York is seen at its best in the distance, as from the approaching liner, when the clusters of shining, metallic buildings as tall and taller than the Eiffel Tower, seem to rise like ascending fountains of beauty. They seem to be some romantic fantasy, specifically calculated to create an emotional effect. They are like mythical Baghdad.'

Cecil Beaton, from *Cecil Beaton's New York* (1938).

NO
TURNS

◇ B ONE
LA

O ↗

URN

NO
URNS

← ONE WAY

◇ TO
BIKE
LANE

WALK TO
← NEXT
SIGN

NO

NYNEX

ITALIAN LIVING DESIGN

In 1930, after three years of construction, a New York landmark opened its doors and launched a new era for Manhattan design. The Chrysler Building has become one of the greatest symbols of New York, a beacon topped by a tiered crown of stainless steel, lit up like a giant radio transmitter beaming across the skyline, echoing the zigzag lines of the crown on the Statue of Liberty. Designed by William van Alen, at 320 metres (1,050 feet) high it was, for just a year, the tallest building in the world until the title was snatched by the Empire State Building, designed by William F. Lamb in 1931. Losing the accolade, though, has never really mattered because the Chrysler Building is still one of the best-loved buildings in New York and one of the greatest icons of Manhattan style.

Van Alen's dream was Manhattan Art Deco at its most perfect and enticing, expressed on the grandest possible scale. The birthplace of Deco might have been Paris, but it grew up in New York. Manhattan Deco swept the city for a decade, falling from the heights of fashion surprisingly quickly yet also attaining a timeless classicism which has helped to define what we now think of as the Manhattan look: a sophisticated, masculine apartment style with an emphasis on neutral restraint, attention to detail, texture and sleek, modern-looking finishes.

The year before the Chrysler Building opened, the Architect and Industrial Arts Exhibition in New York helped carry the message of Deco – perhaps the first genuinely Modernist design movement or decorative style – across the city and across America. Architects such as Josef Urban – a furniture designer as well as a set designer for William Randolph Hearst and the Metropolitan Opera Company – transformed a European style into something distinctly American with their impactive use of geometric patterns, neat utilitarianism and gleaming finishes.

The influences on Deco were many and often exotic: Japanese, Egyptian, North African, French and also Latin American, with the ziggurat profile of Inca and Mayan architecture applied to furniture and buildings alike.

But it was all fused by Urban, Donald Deskey, Paul Frankl and others into something absolutely suited to the new mood of sophisticated, indulgent experimentation that had taken hold of Manhattan.

Manhattan Deco relied on the use of new materials together with an exoticism of design, all refracted through the lens of early Modernist architecture.

Some of these materials were semi-industrial: chrome, especially, but also Bakelite, tubular steel for furniture and reinforced glass for use as bricks, table tops or screens. They were mixed with a common use of lacquer, leather, suede, parquet and other Eastern or more traditional finishes. Fake zebra and leopard skins sometimes added extra fascination and exoticism. At its best Manhattan Deco was moderated by a vein of simplicity and restraint in its form and gently curving lines; at its worst it could tend towards kitsch and extravagance.

Donald Deskey was one of the great Manhattan Deco interior designers. He created many elegant Deco homes and apartments for society New Yorkers such as Abby Aldrich Rockefeller, Helena Rubinstein and the head of Saks Fifth Avenue department store, Adama Gimbel. Most famously in 1932 he created the Deco interiors for the Radio City Music Hall, at the heart of Rockefeller Center, using gilded ceilings, cherrywood panelled walls and a wealth of tubular steel, polished wood and leather. There was an ergonomic modernity to the design which became the talking point of Manhattan.

Other New Yorkers like Russel Wright, Gilbert Rohde and Paul T. Frankl also helped popularize the Deco style with their designs. Frankl was a furniture and interior designer who worked hard to Americanise Deco design, although he was strongly influenced by the Orient with a great love of lacquerware and fine detailing. His skyscraper bookcases and cabinets – echoing the shapes of the many towers springing up like concrete flowers across the city – were essential examples of vogue designer homeware.

The drama and scale of the growing breed of skyscrapers particularly suited Deco, and naturally the designer Manhattan apartment – high above the bustling city streets – assumed a new level of sophisticated style. Deco design was also enthusiastically taken up by Hollywood and applied to films like Cecil B. DeMille's *Dynamite* or *The Kiss* with Greta Garbo. Deco became tied up with the hedonistic exuberance of the Jazz Age, which was given a renewed impetus by the long-awaited end of Prohibition in 1933.

There were many examples of this intense exuberance played out through the medium of design. The grandeur of the Chanin Building (1929) rivalled the nearby Chrysler Building. There were the copper crowns of the Waldorf Astoria (1931) on Park Avenue and also the Daily News Building (1930) on 42nd Street, another Deco landmark towering over the city. They rivalled earlier grand achievements like the Beaux Arts Grand Central Terminal (1913) and the Woolworth Building (1913), fine examples of an earlier pre-war building boom marked by a tendency towards expressive grandeur.

By the 1940s, Manhattan Deco was losing its fashionable appeal and certainly seemed out of place in the context of wartime austerity. But the legacy of Deco lived on and was transformed through the 1940s and 1950s into what we now think of as the classic Manhattan apartment look – a more mature, restrained mixture of Deco elements and a rather more utilitarian and practical form of design, but still

sophisticated, still in many ways luxurious. Silver-leafed tables and cabinets mix with chrome lamps and Deco-style half-barrel chairs. Steel units and floors for kitchens and bathrooms blend with the more luxurious touch of crisp, white towelling and freshly pressed bed linen. Black and white photographs help to decorate the room, rather than paintings or wall hangings, and tailored fabrics of the kind associated with men's suiting, such as flannels and checks, are used for upholstery. The steel-framed furniture remains, often with slung leather which can also used for armchairs and sofas. Suede, too, covers ottomans and low-level seating.

It is a masculine, clean look rooted in the evolving metropolitan modernity of the twentieth century, as opposed to many other more ethnic or rustic design styles.

It is not a look or style associated with pattern and works best with a subdued colour range – greys, ivory whites, taupe and chalky blues. The neutrality of the look – as with Japanese or New England style – allows the texture of materials and finishes to shine through and provides an opportunity to make particular pieces of furniture or artwork into stars. An oversized leather armchair, for instance, or a fine metallic silver cabinet with a dramatic sense of scale assume an extra sense of importance against a more subdued backdrop.

The Manhattan look is about formality, so it doesn't sit well with the rougher edges of Indian or African style. But its neutrality and order does suit certain elements of Chinese and Japanese design. The considered, refined relationship of lacquer and polished surfaces to Deco style carries through into contemporary Manhattan style, where lacquered trunks, shining ceramics and celadon mix quite naturally. Polished bamboo and other elements with natural texture – coir, seagrass, jute for carpets and matting – also sit well the look, tied together by the neutral colourways. And they provide a welcome aspect of contrast with glossier surfaces; there is a real aesthetic power to be had in the juxtaposition of semi-industrial man-made materials with an elegant, considered use of such natural textures. Attention to detail, meanwhile, is always important in the quality of fabrics and fittings.

The rise of the New York loft has helped to further spread the gospel of Manhattan style. Reworking the shells of former industrial spaces has given some lofts a less refined polish with exposed brick, bare wooden floors and bare beams. Yet loft living is at its best within a wholesale adoption of the Manhattan look in all its neutral sophistication, but on the broader canvas of wide open spaces. The sheen of polished wood, sheet steel, lacquer and properly finished surfaces comes alive on such a light, airy stage and there's a real opportunity to give furniture and texture the chance to stand out within the broader dimensions of the loft.

But the loft is not simply about the New York apartment designed on a grander scale, it also involves a different way of living.

The tendency here is towards the growing familiarity of open-plan and multi-functional living spaces, with island kitchens and zones for eating and relaxing, sometimes partitioned off with screens. Bedrooms and bathrooms are tucked away in galleries or separated areas. As with all expressions of the Manhattan look, the loft is an anti-clutter space with a reliance on good storage and ergonomic living that could be applied to many homes without falling into the excesses of minimalism.

Perhaps the greatest impression the growth of the loft has made upon contemporary interior design and architecture is the encouragement of a positive obsession with maximizing light and space in every possible way.

In the city, of course, space is always at a premium, partly explaining the enticement of the loft in the first place. The benefits of open-plan living, vast windows and high ceilings are being applied with varying degrees of success throughout many other sorts of homes and town houses. The use of skylights, glass walls and reflective surfaces – all natural aspects of the Manhattan look – has helped to reinforce the important desire for openness and sunlight, along with internal windows, balconies, and light spiral and steel-framed staircases.

Of course New York, just like the whole of the United States, is a melting pot for design and style as well as a leader in setting fashions and promoting new technologies for the home.

Yet the classic, sleek sophistication of the Manhattan look is an enduring, enticing image. It is rich in so many metropolitan, cultivated associations and will not easily be displaced.

The glamour of Hollywood is highlighted as Sylvia Sydney stands elegantly on a spiral staircase around 1935.

Clark Gable charms Constance Bennett at the barside in Robert Z. Leonard's *After Office Hours* from 1935.

Deco sculptures from Manhattan's Rockefeller Center, the 1930s entertainment complex focused around Radio City Music Hall.

A chrome-surround car clock in 1950s style.

New York's opulent Crown Building, jaggedly reflected in a wall of glass.

Stylized ornamentation on the Chrysler Building.

Skyscrapers dominate the view down Manhattan's long Avenue of the Americas.

A black and white enamel pocket-watch dating from around 1918.

The gleaming simplicity of an Art Deco elevator door in a building on New York's Madison Avenue.

The shapes of Broadway seen through the rain on a cloudy windshield.

Rita Hayworth dances her way through the flamboyant, glamorous sets of the 1946 film *Gilda*, directed by Charles Vidor.

The crown of the Chrysler Building, the most visible glory of Deco Manhattan, was designed by William van Alen and opened its doors in 1930.

A fusion of signage and flashing lights on a New York street points to the vibrancy of everyday Manhattan.

Chrome counter stools sit in front of a soda fountain rich in candy-coloured treats.

Heritage

Heritage is a look of reassuring

associations with a romanticized view of England's past: Richard the Lionheart, Yorkists and Lancastrians, Queen Elizabeth and Sir Francis Drake, Cromwell's Roundheads chasing after Charles I. It is a tradition filtered through Shakespeare and even Hollywood, with Errol Flynn as Robin Hood, and Charles Laughton as Henry VIII. Yet it's a past which still has a hold on us, a past when everything was simpler and uncomplicated. When the country house still had some of the feel of an Englishman's castle, and before the surge of Classicism in the seventeenth century when everything became so much more ornate and complex. It was a time which appealed to the pioneers of the Arts and Crafts Movement of the late nineteenth century, who looked for a medieval kind of simplicity in interior and furniture design. And today the heritage image lives on through heraldic patterns, flagstone floors, bound leather books, great stone fireplaces and the heavy warmth of velvets and chenilles. It is an unrefined, idealistic look, rich in escapism.

There is real sense of warmth to the heritage look.

Inspired by country house style, where the predominant materials were stone and bare wooden panelling, fabrics and colour choices are intended to help raise the temperature and add a sense of comfort. There are heavy cottons and chenilles, together with velvets in fiery reds and glowing yellows, deep blues and strong creams. These fabrics upholster large, welcoming sofas and armchairs set by the fireside, helping to fill large rooms. Paint colours, too, are deep and warm, bringing a sense of intimacy and a touch of heat by association. Rugs and ikats help to soften the floors and heavy curtains line the windows. Here is a reminder that the traditional positioning of

the furniture in a Western room
comes from its relationship to the
fireplace, with the best seats in the
house symmetrically positioned to
surround it. It is a look that places
a particular emphasis on comfort,
while its style is firmly rooted
in tradition.

*The castle is in the very perfection of decay,
all the fine courts, the royal apartments and
rooms of state, lie open and abandoned.
Time, the great devourer of the works of men,
begins to eat into the very stone walls and to
spread the face of royal ruins upon the whole
fabric. Nothing can be added by nature to
make it a place fit for a royal palace. It only
wants the residence of its princes.*

Daniel Defoe, on Ludlow Castle, Shropshire, 'Palace of the Prince of
Wales', from *A Tour Through the Whole Island of Great Britain* (1726).

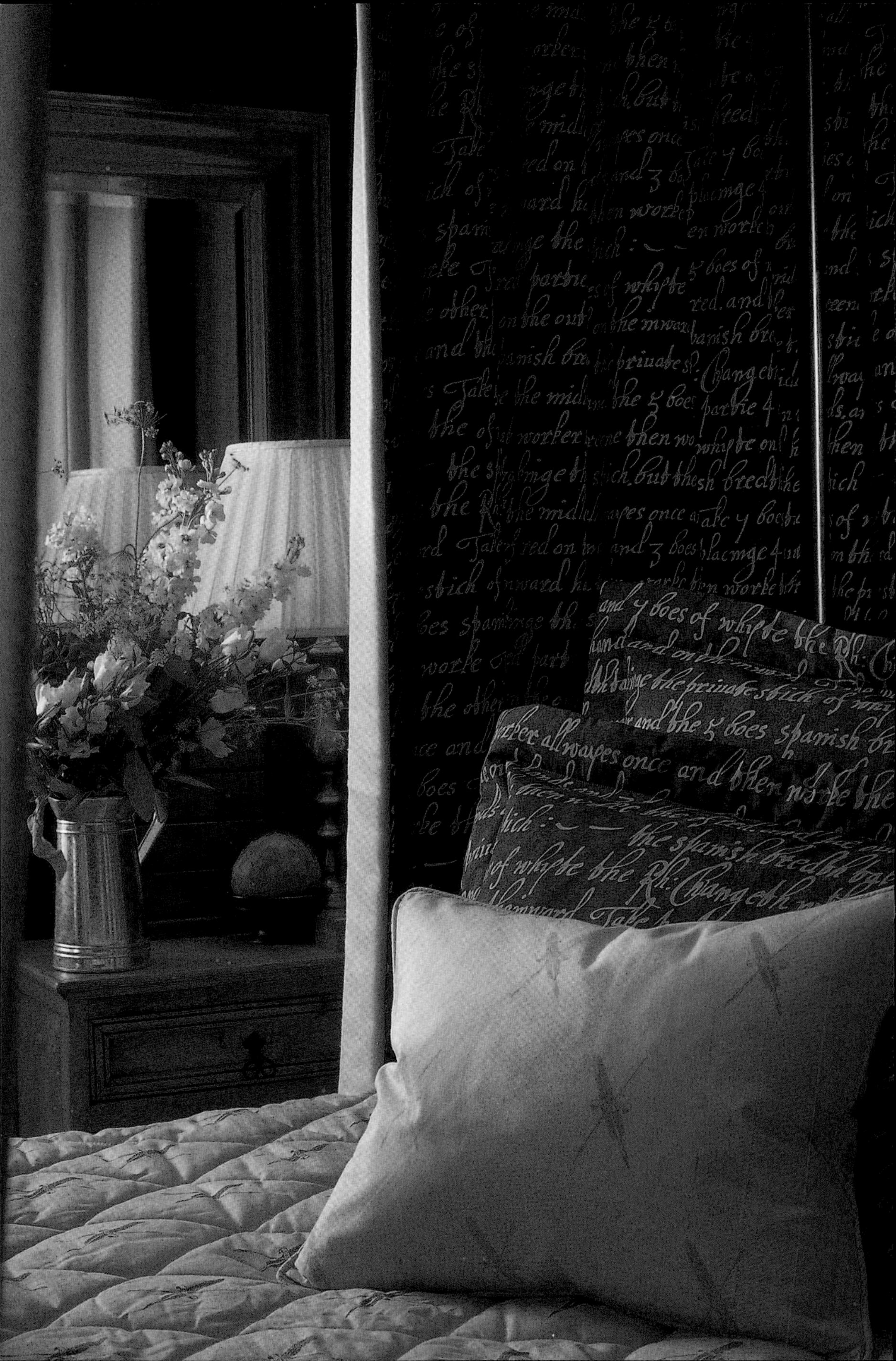

His Roy
Denn
of Engla
Maties Pla

To Lev.^{t}
appointed
Ship the

By Virtue of the Power and Authority
and appoint you ____ Lieutenant of her
Willing and requiring you forthwith to go o
Charge and Comand of ____ Lieutenant in
and Comanding all the Officers and Company
ordinate to you to behave themselves joynt
Imployments with all due respect and obed
And you likewise to observe and execute as n
hereunto annexed. Attested by my Secretary a
you shall from time to time receive from
superior Officers for her Maties Service. H
may faile as you will answer the Contra
doing this shall be your Warrant. Given und
Office of Ld High Admiral this 15th day
yeare of her Maties Reigne.

GEOR

mand of his Royal Highnesse

There is a house in Burwash, Sussex, called Bateman's. It is a Jacobean mansion in honey-shaded stone, covered with creepers, with grounds running down to a small river, complete with water-mill. Rudyard Kipling moved into this house in 1902, with his wife Carrie. 'Behold us now lawful owners of a grey stone lichened house,' he wrote. 'AD 1634 over the door – beamed, panelled, with old oak staircase, and all untouched and unfaked.'

For Kipling, the house was a kind of fantasy turned into reality. Born in India, he had spent much of his life living in the sub-continent or travelling widely and had long felt England to be in many ways foreign to him. He wanted a place where he could settle and stay, somewhere he could really feel at home. That turned out to be Bateman's, where he stayed until his death in 1936, and which also became a creative home to the stories that were collected as *Puck of Pook's Hill* (1906) and *Rewards and Fairies* (1910).

In many ways Bateman's fitted into a romantic dream of Old English style. It offered Kipling the opportunity to play lord of the manor, to escape into and become a part of tradition, to fall in love with the countryside around him to the point where he wrote verses in its honour. The house also fitted in with the emphasis on solid craftsmanship and unadorned simplicity that the architects of the Arts and Crafts Movement had been preaching for the past decade or more. Kipling added pieces from India and others collected on his travels, touches from the East such as Oriental carpets and carvings.

The Jacobean style of Bateman's is all-important. If the house had been built a hundred or perhaps even fifty years later, around the time of the Restoration, its style could have been very different, an example of the extravagance and ornate Classicism of English Baroque that began to really take hold under William and Mary. It was important to Kipling, and perhaps to us, that Bateman's had an elegant simplicity that came of its time.

The sixteenth and early seventeenth centuries form the heartlands of heritage style. They were times of growing political stability during which architects could step away from the necessity of creating fortress architecture and move into a more sophisticated sphere of design while still retaining a rustic, unpolished flavour. They were working in what one might call a true Old England style, beyond the Norman influences perpetuated by the Conquests and before Classicism finally took hold after crossing over from mainland Europe.

It is sometimes hard to remember that before the sixteenth century the great English country house was mostly fortress.

Unrest shaped design and architecture in every way, creating different kinds of defensive enclosures with thick stone walls, small windows and central courtyards. It is the architecture of Kenilworth Castle, dating back to the eleventh century with its layers of walls, grand central keep and great hall. Now in ruins, it inspired Walter Scott's novel *Kenilworth* (1821), and is rich in history as the Warwickshire home of Robert Dudley, Earl of Leicester, favoured courtier of Elizabeth I and potential suitor, whose death in 1588 put the Queen into such a depression that she locked herself in her room. Or look at Middleham Castle in Yorkshire, childhood home to Richard III, built in the twelfth century, with the stone walls of its domineering keep at 3 metres (10 feet) thick. And Arundel Castle in Sussex

– a striking mixture of medieval fortress and Victorian country home, after being remodelled towards the end of the nineteenth century – as well as nearby Bodiam, with its dramatic moat and ramparts.

Throughout the Middle Ages, fortress architecture brought with it a very limited approach to decoration and furnishing, despite the rank and wealth of those few who were able to live on such a scale.

The great hall stood at the centre of the castle home; a place not just for eating but also for talking, entertaining and even sleeping.

Great hooded stone fireplaces would serve to warm the room and the mantelpieces were traditional places for decoration, with carved heraldic symbols showing status and allegiance. And heraldry became increasingly important from the thirteenth century, not simply as an expression of vanity but as a decorative element for mantelpieces, wooden panelling and later stained glass.

The ceiling tended to be simple, with exposed beams. The walls were often plastered to provide some insulation to the large stone rooms. Carpets were valued not so much for the floor, but as wall hangings or ornate table decorations. Tapestry was common by the fourteenth century, a warmer and more colourful alternative to paintings and portraiture. Tapestry, too, was a status symbol as so much of it was originally imported from France and the Low Countries, designed with religious episodes, hunting scenes and images of battle and courtly love. Furniture was scarce, dining tables and beds among the most significant pieces.

And it was beds rather than windows which were likely to be curtained with tapestries and other hangings to help keep out the cold.

Through the centuries there was a gradual development in ornament and decoration, a slow growth of interest in colour and pattern. Wooden panelling, or wainscoting, was increasingly used to cover bare stone walls and was sometimes painted, as was plasterwork. Murals and simple patterns, such as fleur-de-lys, became increasingly popular, not only among the aristocrats but also the growing merchant classes. Colours became more varied, with the use of rich reds, blues, even gold. Henry III's favourite colour was supposedly green, which he requested more than once for the decoration of Winchester Castle in the thirteenth century.

Tiled floors were common by the fourteenth century and the choice of textiles gradually became richer, much of it imported — linens, cotton and silk, velvet from Italy — although wool was always the most common and easily available. Finely produced embroidery, such as opus anglicanum, became important in the thirteenth and fourteenth centuries and was exported across Europe.

By the sixteenth century architecture and design began to move to a new level of accomplishment and skill. The rise of the Tudors brought greater stability and therefore more freedom in developing a true English domestic architecture without worrying about the necessity of defence. At the same time, Henry VIII's break with Rome in the 1530s served to partly isolate England throughout the century, and even beyond, from the growing importance of Renaissance style and the rise of architectural Classicism. While the sixteenth century saw a surge in building and architecture – partly funded by the dissolution of the monasteries, with ecclesiastical buildings pulled apart to help build private homes – it also offered a chance to develop a more genuine English style way beyond the Norman influence. It was a rich time of transition between medieval primitivism and a more cultivated approach, which forms a focal point for heritage style.

The English country house was redesigned, moving away from the centralism of the great hall towards what we think of as a more traditional and familiar floor plan with greater importance given to symmetry.

Away went the exposed beams and vaulted ceiling and in came panelled wooden ceilings, sometimes carved and ornamented or decorated with geometric plaster mouldings. Wainscoting became very common for the walls, sometimes even from floor to ceiling, and was either lightly patterned, carved or painted. Fireplaces became more elaborate, a true symbol of wealth and status. Glass was now in more widespread use and so windows became larger and features in themselves, allowing light to play

around the interior, while stained glass used heraldic images, multicoloured patterns and sometimes even more complex designs.

Tudor manor houses such as Barrington Court in Somerset, Coughton Court in Warwickshire and Elizabethan glories such as Sizergh Castle, Cumbria, and Wakehurst Place in Sussex suggest the breadth and scale of the sixteenth century's architectural legacy. The restraint of early Tudor style gradually gave way to a more flamboyant approach to decoration under Elizabeth, with craftsmanship quickly progressing in paintwork, carving in stone and wood, as well as in the increasingly complex methods and manner of plasterwork. Colours became richer and warmer: oranges, yellows, russet reds and popinjay (a mix of green and blue). Wallpaper came into use, with many of the early patterns simply imitating the look of fabrics or using heraldic imagery. Wooden floors became common, and window shutters were seen as more practical than curtains.

At the start of the seventeenth century, under James I, the influence of Classicism slowly began to make its presence felt. Throughout the Jacobean era, the East became more important as a reference point, with the use of Arabesques in decorative painting and a growing accessibility of silks, cottons and the exotic brilliance of Chinese crafts. But we still associate Jacobean style with aspects of medievalism mixed with a widespread use of oak and carved wood – heavy staircases and dark dining tables, chairs and panels. The first decades of the century saw a continuation of building in a broadly Old English style, with the relative modesty of houses such as Chastleton House in Oxfordshire and Bateman's at one end of the spectrum and then the romantic grandeur of Bolsover Castle, Derbyshire, or Audley End in Essex – created on the scale of a royal palace by the Earl of Suffolk, Treasurer to James I – at the other end.

By the end of the seventeenth century, though, English architecture had been transformed by the influence of Classicism, of Christopher Wren and Inigo Jones, who energetically promoted Palladian style. This was a very different approach to architecture compared to that of Tudor and even Jacobean England, a finer approach and – as English Baroque began to reach its zenith in the 1680s and 1690s – also an excessive one, in its great love of flamboyance and ornament.

The heritage look is grounded in that restrained Old English style of the Tudor era and the early Jacobean age.

It looks to a time before the lessons of the Renaissance really struck, before the arrival of excess, a time when the home was 'beamed, panelled, with old oak staircase, and all untouched' as Kipling put it. Colours are warm but faded, as if through time, and fabric patterns use heraldic symbols, old-fashioned calligraphy texts and charters, royal lions and unicorns.

Escapist touches come through the types of items you imagine discovering in a cobwebbed country attic: painted family crests and old portraits, leather-bound books and trunks, ancient toys in painted wood.

Other elements with traditional English associations creep into the mix, such as leather suitcases used decoratively, cricket bats and brass telescopes – unexpected elements with stories all their own, adding extra twists of interest to the room. Other upholstery fabrics might use postal motifs and seals. More architectural elements, such as stone garden urns and pinnacles, add texture and impact through their scale and by being so out of context. Floors tend to be wood or stone, but with the choice of extra warmth through underfloor heating. The references are not fine or cosmopolitan, but rustic and even archaic, tied up with faded grandeur and the legacies of English traditionalism.

The Arts and Crafts Movement of the late nineteenth century had a similar sense of fascination with medieval and pre-Classical architecture and design. They romanticized the heritage look in their own way, seeing in it an honest, well-crafted and unpretentious aesthetic which brought with it a simpler way of living. 'Instead of painting boughs of apple trees on our door panels and covering every shelf with petticoats of silk,' wrote Charles Voysey in 1893, 'let us begin by discarding the mass of useless ornaments and banishing the millinery that degrades our furniture and fittings.' A little strong, you might think, but indicative of a fascination with the kind of house, the kind of home living, that Kipling adopted at Bateman's a few years later.

William Morris, the premier of the Arts and Crafts Movement, made Kelmscott Manor in Oxfordshire his home from 1871 until his death in 1896. A gabled Cotswold-stone house, it was, of course, Elizabethan and fitted in not just with his philosophical approach but also with his textile designs. Made up as wall hangings, they blended perfectly with the stone fireplaces, wooden panelling and heavy pieces of Jacobean-style furniture. Other architects and designers associated with the Movement – such as Voysey and Frank Dickinson – also created semi-medieval homes for themselves, living the design as well as preaching it.

Throughout the twentieth century there have been resurgences of the Old English or heritage style from time to time.

Lord Moyne, an MP and member of the Guinness brewing family, recreated a mock Tudor settlement on the Sussex coast in the 1920s and named it Bailiffscourt, mixing genuine medieval buildings – moved onto the estate stone by stone – with other sympathetic modern reconstructions. In New York one of the most charismatic buildings in the city is now a medieval folly. Funded by John D. Rockefeller Jr. as a branch of The Metropolitan Museum devoted to European art of the Middle Ages, the Cloisters was built in the late 1930s among the gardens and trees of Fort Tryon Park. Five genuine medieval cloisters form part of the modern structure created in period style, with the joins almost seamless, at a time when sophisticated Deco extravagance was all the rage across Manhattan.

A contemporary expression of Heritage style, on a more modest scale, also relies on restraint and simple elegance.

The temptation might be to go too far, to create a pastiche filled with ephemera. That would be to undermine the look and its tone of cultivated moderation. But it is a look which suits the country, and its rustic, unrefined element fits in with more informal aspects of fusion interiors. The rough edges of Indian and South East Asian furniture partner the heritage theme well, as do ikats, kilims or Indian dhurries for a touch of pattern and colour. Elements of Safari style, too, sit neatly with the mix: statuary and wooden carvings along with the natural textures of seagrass or coir.

Part of the point of heritage style is its informality and it does not sit naturally with a more cosmopolitan look such as Manhattan, or the more finished and refined aspects of Japanese and Chinese design.

Throughout this book we have looked at aspects of fusion design which veer either towards a more formal approach or a more relaxed outlook. Clearly it is always better to decide which is more appropriate given the way you want to live and where you live – country or city, modern or period home.

END NOTE: IN FUSION

The principles of fusion interiors are broad and are all about maximizing choices, not denying them. Sometimes contrasts between more formal design elements and rougher textures or finishes can work, as with juxtapositions of Chinese or Japanese design with the less polished craftsmanship of South East Asian style. However, the more disparate the elements that you are bringing together in one place, the greater the care needed to find a common thread between them.

Colour is always the most obvious solution and can often provide enough of a link, but texture and approaches to pattern – including the exclusion of pattern – are also important for creating a common currency within a room and should not be neglected.

Such diverse elements as Inca, Raj, Heritage and others might at first seem quite separate and distinct. Yet there are recurring themes that come up again and again. Throughout all these elements of fusion style there is an emphasis on an appreciation of good design – whether it is rustic, ethnic or quite cosmopolitan in its character – and also considered design which gives an equal value to form and function.

Craftsmanship, too, is all-important whether in attention to detail and finish or in the hope that we can find through the crafted object or particular pattern some connection with the hand or culture that made it. Restraint, simplicity and quality, too, are all keys to the whole idea of fusion interiors.

And while the style and elegance of the fusion look has a decidedly contemporary feel in the way we bring these different ideas together, at the same time we are always looking back to other cultures and traditions, to the arts and crafts of disappearing tribes and lost empires. We are building on a legacy of design from all parts of the world and looking for something old as well as new. Through colour, texture, pattern and design the look of fusion style is rich in associations with other countries and cultures, with the experiences, people and sights of our travels both in reality and imagination. And through those associations we return to the importance not just of style, elegance and comfort, but of the vitality and necessity of escapism in the home.

Coats of arms decorate a portico at Felbrigg Hall, Norfolk – one of the finest seventeenth-century country houses in the area.

A shrub grows up along the line of worn steps at Bodnant Garden in Gwynedd, Wales.

The sun on this bell tower evokes Rupert Brookes' classic image of England's countryside.

The age of leisurely ocean travel seems a world away from the hectic dash of today's airports. Now tin trunks are better used for attractive storage in the house.

After the match – a cricket team pictured on the steps of a pavilion in 1863.

An engraving from 1810 by Thomas Sutherland of Saint George's Chapel, Windsor Castle, with heraldic flags and intricately carved choir stalls.

A 1705 letter of appointment signed by Prince George of Denmark, Lord High Admiral of England.

Panelling and doorway at The Vyne, Hampshire, built in the early sixteenth century by William, 1st Lord Sandys.

Early twentieth-century lead toy soldiers combine a high level of crafsmanship with an image of half-forgotten childhood, which is appealing for collectors today.

Officers of the 1st Suffolk regiment pictured in their uniforms in 1895.

Seventeenth-century England had a simplicity of design that has a deep resonance four hundred years later.

A collection of copper pans and moulds in the kitchen of Brodsworth Hall, Yorkshire.

A Chinese willow pattern plate sits above a carved oak frieze at Chastleton House, Oxfordshire, which is often described as one of England's finest and most unspoiled Jacobean houses.

The present Duke of Devonshire asleep in his library at Chatsworth in Derbyshire, which

BIBLIOGRAPHY

Patricia Bayer, *Art Deco Interiors* (Thames and Hudson, 1990)

Tim Beddow & Natasha Burns, *Safari Style* (Thames and Hudson, 1998)

Monisha Bharadwaj, *Inside India* (Kyle Cathie, 1998)

Ettagale Blauer, *African Elegance* (New Holland, 1999)

Patricia Buckley Ebrey, *China* (Cambridge University Press, 1996)

William Dalrymple (foreword), *Sacred India* (Lonely Planet, 1999)

Jane Edwards & Andrew Wood, *Asian Elements* (Conran Octopus, 1999)

Charlotte & Peter Fiell, *Design of the 20th Century* (Taschen, 1999)

Wendell Garrett, *American Colonial* (Evergreen, 1998)

Jonathan Glancey, *20th Century Architecture* (Carlton, 1998)

Alan & Ann Gore, *The History of English Interiors* (Phaidon, 1991)

Adrianna von Hagen & Craig Morris, *The Cities of the Ancient Andes* (Thames and Hudson, 1998)

Dinah Hall, *Ethnic by Design* (Mitchell Beazley, 1992)

Luca Invernizzi Tettoni, *Tropical Asian Style* (Evergreen, 1998)

Barbara Lloyd, *The Colours of Southern India* (Thames and Hudson, 1999)

Lisa Lovatt-Smith, *Moroccan Interiors* (Taschen, 1995)

Anne Massey, *Interior Design of the 20th Century* (Thames and Hudson, 1990)

Edward S. Morse, *Japanese Homes and their Surroundings* (Sampson Low, Marston, Searle and Rivington, 1886)

Kate Muir (ed.), *Writers and their Houses* (Hamish Hamilton, 1993)

Eric Newby (ed.), *A Book of Traveller's Tales* (Picador, 1985)

Deidi von Schaewen & Sunil Sethi, *Indian Interiors* (Taschen, 1999)

Suzanne Slesin & Stafford Cliff, *Indian Style* (Thames and Hudson, 1990)

Suzanne Slesin, Stafford Cliff & Daniel Rozensztroch, *Japanese Style* (Thames and Hudson, 1987)

Suzanne Slesin, Stafford Cliff & Daniel Rozensztroch, *New York Style* (Thames and Hudson, 1992)

Henri Stierlin, *Hindu India* (Taschen, 1998)

Henri Stierlin, *The Maya* (Taschen, 1997)

Beate Wedekind, *New York Interiors* (Taschen, 1997)

Elizabeth Wilhide & Joanna Copestick, *Modern Exotic* (Conran Octopus, 1999)

ANDREW MARTIN AGENTS AND DISTRIBUTORS

UK
ANDREW MARTIN
SHOWROOM
200 Walton Street
London SW3 2JL
+44 20 7225 5100

US DISTRIBUTOR
Kravet Fabrics
225 Central Avenue
South Bethpage
NY 11714
+1 516 293 2000
or call
(888) 4-KRAVET
for showrooms in
your local area

**OTHER
DISTRIBUTORS:**
ARGENTINA
Miranda Green
+11 4 802 0850

AUSTRALIA
Unique Fabrics
+61 3 98 16 2000

AUSTRIA
Designers Details
+43 1 533 4047

BELGIUM
Intede
+32 2 513 0261

BERMUDA
Howe Enterprises
+1 441 292 1433

BRAZIL
Miranda Green
+11 4 802 0850

CANADA
Kravet
+1 416 921 1262

CHILE
Patricia Vargas
+56 2 228 7682

CYPRUS
Sit Kyros Cyprus
+357 2 314 000

DENMARK
Classics Halker
+45 98 669 282

EGYPT
Artissimo
+20 3 422 88 50

FINLAND
Naccanil
+358 9 587 30 66

FRANCE
Pierre Frey
+33 1 44 77 36 00

GIBRALTAR
Nappa Holdings
+350 952 81 79 36

GERMANY
Hahne & Schonberg
+49 89 542 77 30

GREECE
Kyros Group
+30 1 662 68 22

HONG KONG
Kinsan
+852 252 623 09

HUNGARY
Dekor Classic
+36 1 342 27 20

INDONESIA
Jesindo
+62 31 594 0000

IRELAND
Furnishing
Distributors
+353 1 283 3743

ISRAEL
Loft Furniture
+972 9 9582 8206

ITALY
Decortex
+390 55 887 3093

JORDAN
Elba Jordanian
+962 6 566 5948

KENYA
Spiegel
+254 2 762 762

KOREA
Heimtextil
+82 2 546 0166

KUWAIT
Euro-Diwan
+965 476 7743

LATVIA
Interior Design
+371 7283 804

LEBANON
Linea Verde
+961 1 422 456

MALAYSIA
Oakleaf Interior
+60 3 470 1798

MEXICO
Comernet
+52 8 336 7 339

MOROCCO
Rodesma
+212 2 29 72 94

NETHERLANDS
Chivasso
+31 79 360 1111

NEW ZEALAND
Unique
+64 9 306 15 80

NORWAY
Poesi
+47 22 55 00 30

PERU
Punto Fiamma
+51 1 421 5999

PHILIPPINES
Shell Canvas
+63 2 867 1994

PORTUGAL
Pinto & Barreiros
+351 22 948 5022

RUSSIA
Artistic Design
+7 095 203 3397

SAUDI ARABIA
The Gallery
+966 3 896 1469

SINGAPORE
Just the Place
+65 7353 389

SOUTH AFRICA
Halogen
+27 11 448 2060

SPAIN
Alhambra
+34 96 593 2095

SWEDEN
Interior Plus
+46 8 665 3118

SWITZERLAND
Seilaz
+41 1 422 14 01

TAIWAN
Pillota
+886 2 271 76178

TURKEY
Andrew Martin
+90 212 296 13 0

Photographs showing some of the Andrew Martin Collections:

Tang Hessian from the Andrew Martin Qin Collection

Abaca cloth from the Crusoe Collection

Band from the Kelly Hoppen Collection

Antique hide with Gobi band from the Explorer Collection

Pride from the Naivasha Collection

Mungo Park from the Explorer Collection

Sabir from the Tamerlane Collection

Patagonia from the Havana Collection with Molesuede

Andes & Llama from the Inca Collection

Inti & Aztec from the Inca Collection

Cuzco from the Inca Collection

Jehangir from the Mughal Collection

Mahal from the Mughal Collection

Akbar from the Mughal Collection

Berber from the Mughal Collection

July from the Carolyn Quartermaine Collection

Palmerston Linen from the First Post Collection

Tajik from the Tamerlane Collection

Lawn Stripe with the July from the Carolyn Quartermaine Collection

Excalibur from the Crusader Collection

"Rhino" leather from the Rawhide Collection

Lionheart from the Conqueror Collection

Riverpoint from the Nantucket Collection

Cannes Damask velvet with Jupiter Silk cushion

Revolution from the Meridian Collection

Legend and Guinevere from the Calligraphy Collection

Invention from the Meridian Collection

Magna Carta from the Conqueror Collection

Prince of Wales Check from the Brummel Collection

Ivanhoe from the Crusader Collection

Avignon Collection

Titan and Hyperion from the Titan Collection